Majesty

Reflections on the life of Christ
with Queen Elizabeth II

RICHARD HARRIES

First published in Great Britain in 2023

SPCK
RH101
The Record Hall
16–16A Baldwin's Gardens
London EC1N 7RJ
www.spck.org.uk

British Library Cataloguing-in-Publication Data
A catalogue record for this book is available from the British Library

ISBN 978–0–281–08947–5
eBook ISBN 978–0–281–08948–2

1 3 5 7 9 10 8 6 4 2

Typeset by Fakenham Prepress Solutions, Fakenham, Norfolk NR21 8NL

First printed by Dream Colour (Hong Kong) Printing Ltd

eBook by Fakenham Prepress Solutions, Fakenham, Norfolk NR21 8NL

Produced on paper from sustainable sources

To the people of St Mary's, Barnes

Contents

Introduction

Everyone anticipated that when Her Majesty Queen Elizabeth II one day died there would be a great sense of loss, but the extent and depth of the national grief when she did so was quite extraordinary. So many people clearly felt a personal connection with her and experienced a sense of personal loss. Even staunch republicans recognized and praised her outstanding personal qualities. She inherited those qualities above all from her father.

As a teenage member of my school cadet corps in 1952 I was one of many in uniform lining the route of the 3-mile Long Walk up to Windsor Castle. I stood there, rifle reversed and pointing downwards, eyes lowered, when, to the sound of slow drum beat, the cortège of the late King George VI passed slowly by. There was one word in particular in 1952 which characterized the best of that generation, as displayed so notably by George VI: duty. You were expected to do your duty, to God, to the country and, if you were a citizen, to the monarch. That word seems to have dropped out of current usage. But Her Majesty the Queen took it from her father and revealed its reality and crucial importance over 70 changing and challenging years.

To do one's duty is to accept the responsibilities of the role one inhabits – as a parent to a child, as children to parents, as citizens to the country, as employers to employees, and vice versa, as Christians to the church to which we belong. To accept the responsibilities of a role is to put aside one's personal feelings, one's likes and dislikes, to do what the role requires. It involves daily sacrifice. We saw this pre-eminently in our much-loved late Queen. She did not ask to be monarch, certainly not at that young age. But from the first she recognized that it was a responsibility she had to accept and from the first she pledged herself to fulfil its duties, which she did faithfully to the end. Her life was one given over to service.

That steadfast faithfulness was rooted in her Christian faith, as was made increasingly clear in the royal broadcasts of recent years. It wasn't pushed in your face, it did not make those without faith feel uncomfortable, but it was clearly real, and at the heart of her life of service to the country. If she had been asked what that faith was, I suspect she would have directed us to the two great commandments – to love God with all that we are, and our neighbours as ourselves. As she put it in her Christmas broadcast in 2012:

This is the time of year when we remember that God sent his only Son 'to serve, and not to be served'. He restored love and service to the centre of our lives in the person of Jesus Christ.

That service included her role in relation to the Church of England, which again she faithfully carried out. She opened every new synod of the Church of England. She appeared at numerous big services in cathedrals round the country; she invited every diocesan bishop once in their tenure of office to stay with her for a weekend at Sandringham. There were huge changes during the Queen's reign and she changed some of what she did in order to be more in touch, but there was one area where people did not seem to want the monarch to be like them. As Graham James, a former Bishop of Norwich, has put it:

> When I observed the huge crowds at Sandringham watching the Queen go to church, it was clear that they did not expect that she might have a lie-in that Sunday. The Queen seemed to do a lot of vicarious churchgoing for the nation.

The word duty seems too stern for our tastes today, but in the late Queen it went with a great sense of humour and fun. I love the story from a time at Balmoral – a place where she could be informal – when she popped into the local shop. A woman came in, looked at her and said, 'You look very like the Queen.' 'How very reassuring,' the Queen replied. It was a humour which revealed her underlying humility. At a meeting of the Privy Council someone's mobile phone rang. As they fumbled to turn it off the Queen looked at them and said, 'Hadn't you better answer it? It might be someone important.'

She was always alert to what was going on. At the Sandringham weekend the visiting bishop preaches at the local church on the Sunday morning. When I did it, the lesson was read rather well by a member of the congregation and after the service a group, including the Queen and myself, gathered round her to congratulate her. Looking at me, the Queen suddenly said, 'You weren't listening, Bishop.' Like many a nervous preacher I had taken the opportunity to have a surreptitious look at my notes during the lesson. 'I was doing both, Ma'am,' I replied. She missed nothing.

One of the aspects of her role that the Queen performed so well was to be both a serious member of the Church of England and a monarch for all faiths, and in doing so she both reflected and reinforced a vital part played by her church over the past 70 years. As she told bishops in 2012, the Church

> certainly provides an identity and spiritual dimension for its own many adherents. But also, gently and assuredly, the Church of England has created an environment for other faith communities and indeed people of no faith to live freely. Woven into the fabric of this country, the Church has helped to build a better society – more and more in active co-operation for the common good with those of other faiths.

This book, written out of a deep sense of respect and gratitude to Her Majesty, consists of four elements: first, extracts from the life and teachings of Jesus to be found in the Gospels; second, scenes from the life of Christ as portrayed in paintings from the Royal Collection and elsewhere; third, reflections on how the artists have depicted the scenes; fourth, quotations from Her Majesty's Christmas broadcasts which relate her faith to that life of Christ and his teachings.

The magnificent Royal Collection of paintings and other works of art contains a fair number on biblical subjects. I have selected 20 of these on the life of Christ and added another 30 from other sources to tell the story of his birth, life,

death and resurrection. Those selected come from a variety of periods and reflect different forms of Christian art.

The poet laureate, Simon Armitage, has written a lovely poem comparing the Queen to a lily whose brightness will continue to glow. For Christians, that brightness will hold and glow beyond the border of this mortal life. For so many of us it will continue to glow in lives lit anew by her wonderful example. This book hopes to bring something of the source and inspiration of that life to the fore.

Richard Harries

Majesty

1
LIGHT OF THE WORLD

'St Paul spoke of the first Christmas as the kindness of God dawning upon the world. The world needs that kindness now more than ever.'

The Queen's Christmas broadcast, 1997

DETAIL FROM
**THE ADORATION OF
THE SHEPHERDS**
Jacopo Bassano (1510–92)
King's drawing room,
Kensington Palace

The annunciation

In the sixth month, the angel Gabriel was sent by God to a town in Galilee called Nazareth, to a virgin engaged to a man whose name was Joseph, of the house of David. The virgin's name was Mary. And he came to her and said, 'Greetings, favoured one! The Lord is with you.' But she was much perplexed by his words and pondered what sort of greeting this might be. The angel said to her, 'Do not be afraid, Mary, for you have found favour with God. And now, you will conceive in your womb and bear a son, and you will name him Jesus. He will be great, and will be called the Son of the Most High, and the Lord God will give to him the throne of his ancestor David. He will reign over the house of Jacob for ever, and of his kingdom there will be no end.' Mary said to the angel, 'How can this be, since I am a virgin?' The angel said to her, 'The Holy Spirit will come upon you, and the power of the Most High will overshadow you; therefore the child to be born will be holy; he will be called Son of God. And now, your relative Elizabeth in her old age has also conceived a son; and this is the sixth month for her who was said to be barren. For nothing will be impossible with God.' Then Mary said, 'Here am I, the servant of the Lord; let it be with me according to your word.' Then the angel departed from her.

From the Gospel of Luke, chapter 1

THE ANNUNCIATION
Carlo Maratti (1625–1713)
Queen's private chapel,
Hampton Court Palace

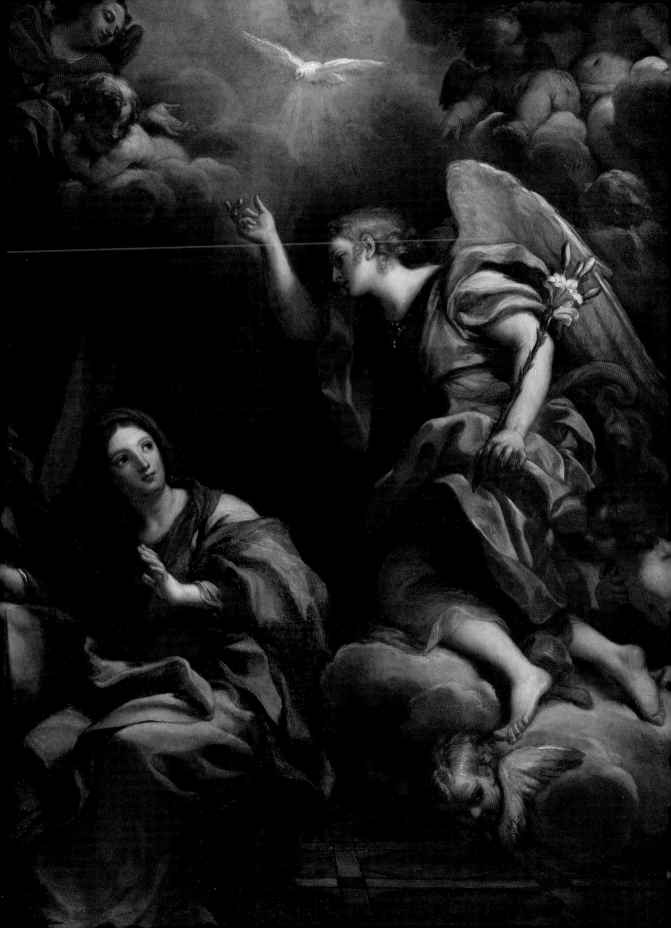

The annunciation was depicted in the fifth century, in a mosaic, and may even have been painted earlier than this in the catacombs. By the time of Fra Angelico in the fifteenth century it was a familiar scene in art. Fra Angelico was a monk and his version exudes quiet prayerfulness.

The version here by Maratti could not be more different. It is dramatic, even theatrical. The angel Gabriel, a towering figure with right arm raised, appears overpowering. Angels and putti are all around but almost pushed aside. Mary to the left looks up at him with a sense of surprise and questioning. Gabriel carries a white lily, the traditional symbol of Mary, who wears blue, her traditional colour, and is shown reading a book. It is open at Isaiah 7.14–16 (AV): 'Therefore the Lord himself shall give you a sign; Behold, a virgin shall conceive, and bear a son, and shall call his name Immanuel.'

The Holy Spirit, symbolized as a dove, overshadows Mary. The face of God the Father in outline looms above – which is incorrect theologically. According to Christian theology, God in himself is totally unknown and incomprehensible so should not be depicted in art. But God has made himself known in a way that we humans can understand, in Jesus, the Word made flesh. It is his life that justifies Christian art.

Maratti's version reflects two main influences, one religious and the other artistic. In response to the Protestant Reformation, the Roman Catholic Church made strenuous attempts to reform its life, known as the Counter-Reformation.

Religious orders were founded and missionaries went all over the world, inspired with a new zeal. Their preaching was dramatic, and they used theatre to get their message across. Although Maratti stood in the Classical tradition of Raphael, he was influenced by the much more flamboyant Baroque art. It is an art designed to depict, and get the viewer to share, strong emotions. So one of its features is light and glory, very much to the fore here with light breaking through the clouds and lighting up the darkness below. And it is right for it to be dramatic, for what could be more astounding than the Eternal Word taking form as a human person? What more glorious than Eternal Love sharing human vulnerability?

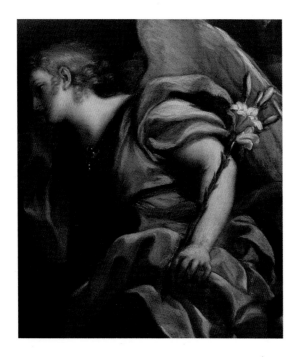

The angel Gabriel, a towering figure with right arm raised, appears overpowering.

The visitation

In those days Mary set out and went with
haste to a Judean town in the hill country,
where she entered the house of Zechariah
and greeted Elizabeth. When Elizabeth heard
Mary's greeting, the child leapt in her womb.
And Elizabeth was filled with the Holy Spirit
and exclaimed with a loud cry, 'Blessed are you
among women, and blessed is the fruit of your
womb. And why has this happened to me, that
the mother of my Lord comes to me? For as soon
as I heard the sound of your greeting, the child
in my womb leapt for joy. And blessed is she who
believed that there would be a fulfilment of what
was spoken to her by the Lord.'
From the Gospel of Luke, chapter 1

VISITATION
Rogier van der Weyden
(1399/1400–1464)
Museum of Fine Arts, Leipzig

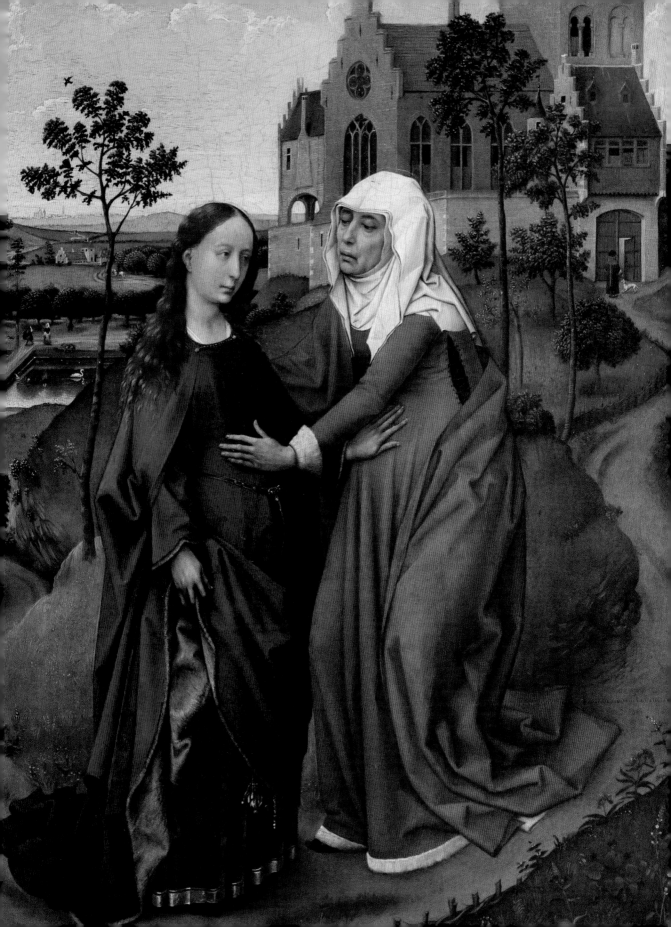

This painting by the Netherlandish artist Rogier
van der Weyden picks up a number of details
from the biblical account. It is hilly, for example,
and a long journey is suggested by the panoramic
views and people on the path some distance
away. There is a small figure by the building
playing with a dog; the figure is assumed to
be the husband of Elizabeth, Zechariah. The
biblical account says Mary entered his house, but
in this depiction the greeting takes place outside.
Mary is in her traditional blue. Elizabeth, with
an older face, bends down slightly. Each woman
places their hands tenderly on the stomach of the
other, conscious of the vulnerability of the child
within and the vulnerability of the mother as
they look to giving birth with all its risks. In the
biblical narrative Elizabeth's child leaps for joy in
the womb, reflecting the precedence which John
the Baptist will accord to Jesus in the subsequent
narratives. Jesus is the bridegroom, John the best
man who rejoices in the presence of the groom,
and already in the womb that rejoicing begins.

For people in our time this scene is above all
a depiction of the support women have given
one another down the ages. As soon as Mary
heard the amazing, disturbing news that she was
to give birth to God's specially chosen one she
rushed off to her cousin. The narrative says she
stayed with her for three months. In a brutal,
male-dominated world such female friendship has
so often been the only support.

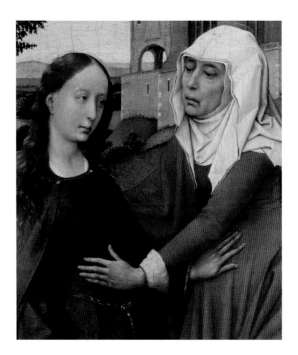

Mary is in her traditional blue. Elizabeth, with an older face, bends down slightly. Each woman places their hands tenderly on the stomach of the other, conscious of the vulnerability of the child within and the vulnerability of the mother as they look to giving birth with all its risks.

The birth of Jesus

In those days a decree went out from Emperor Augustus that all the world should be registered. This was the first registration and was taken while Quirinius was governor of Syria. All went to their own towns to be registered. Joseph also went from the town of Nazareth in Galilee to Judea, to the city of David called Bethlehem, because he was descended from the house and family of David. He went to be registered with Mary, to whom he was engaged and who was expecting a child. While they were there, the time came for her to deliver her child. And she gave birth to her firstborn son and wrapped him in bands of cloth, and laid him in a manger, because there was no place for them in the inn.

From the Gospel of Luke, chapter 2

In this traditional icon Mary lies on a pallet, exhausted after childbirth, bringing out the reality of this human birth. But she is in the centre of the picture, the divine shaft of light coming down on the babe beside her, angels above and human scenes below, heaven and earth united in her son. Western art depicts the birth in a stable, but Orthodox art in a cave and that is what visitors to Bethlehem are shown. The mountains are bare and rocky but in them green shoots are beginning to grow, the first sign of the new creation in Christ.

The angels bow in reverence to the Christ-child. Below are two scenes that appear not in the Bible but in icons. To the left, a glum Joseph is tempted by a figure in a sheepskin not to believe in the miraculous conception of the babe. To the right, two midwives help to wash the child. This scene was taken over from classical antiquity, for in Paphos in Cyprus a similar scene appears for the birth of Dionysius and in Beirut for the birth of Alexander the Great. The appearance of the two midwives is derived from a second-century document, the *Protoevangelium of James*, in which they witness to the fact that Mary was indeed *virgo intacta*.

One much-loved scene in early and medieval art was that of the animals bending over the crib to worship the child in their way. Their presence is due to Isaiah 1.3: 'The ox knows its owner, and the donkey its master's crib; but Israel does not know, my people do not understand.'

NATIVITY OF THE LORD (ICON)
Andrei Rublev (1360s to between 1427 and 1430)
Cathedral of the Annunciation, Moscow

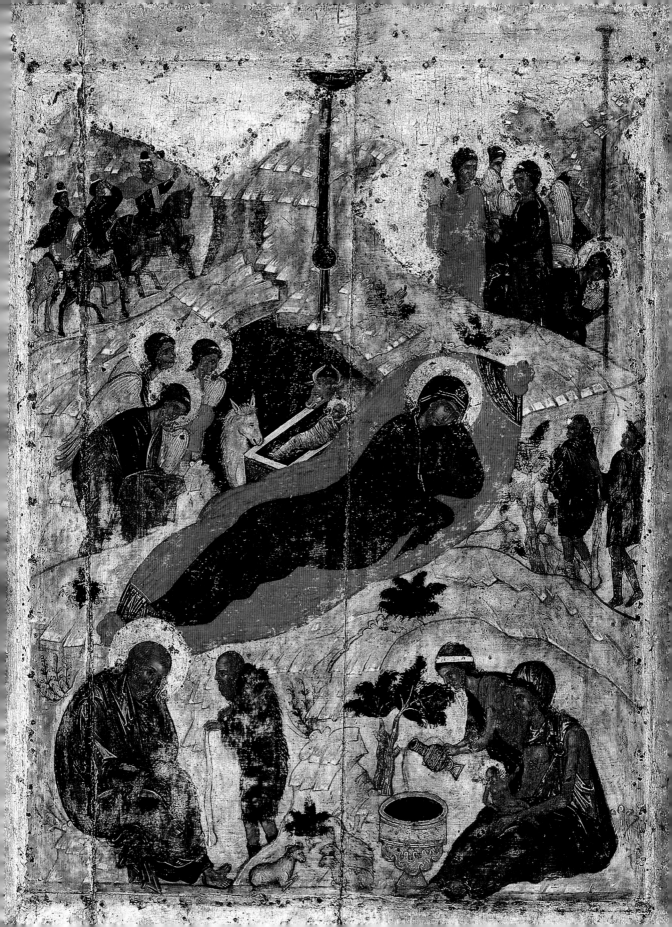

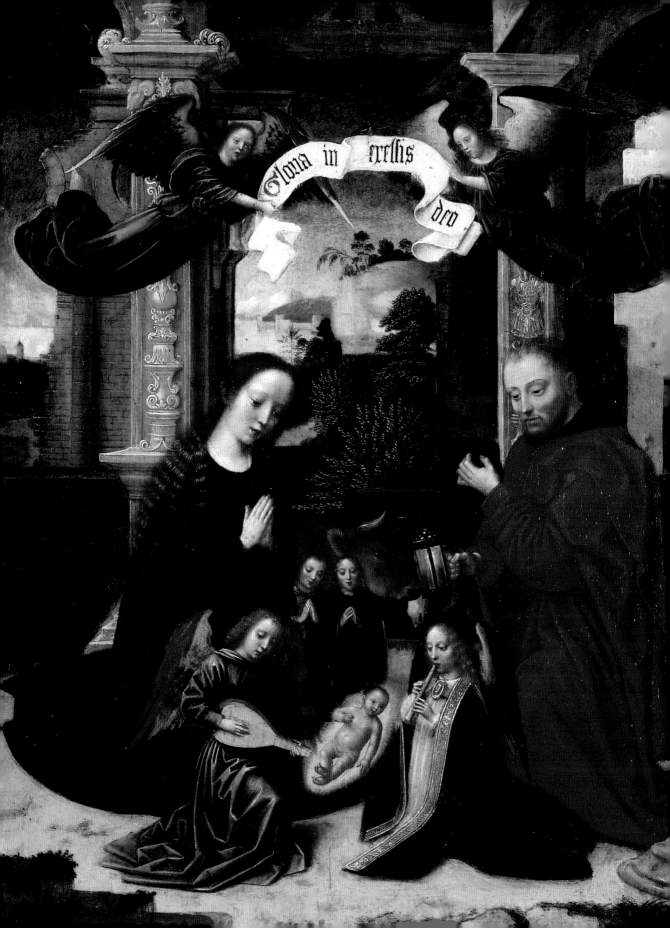

In 2017, Her Majesty the Queen reflected:

'We remember the birth of Jesus Christ whose only sanctuary was a stable in Bethlehem. He knew rejection, hardship and persecution; and yet it is Jesus Christ's generous love and example which has inspired me through good times and bad.'

This work is one of several simply signed GB. It is not certain who this is, hence it is assigned to GB monogrammist. It is thought it may be by Guillaume Benson, an artist documented in Bruges, a great centre of Netherlands art at a great time, between 1544 and late 1574. Even if GB does not stand for Benson it is still probable from the style of the works that they were painted in Bruges at this time. It depicts a quiet scene of just the intimate family and angels. It brings to mind a time in the lives of new parents when all the visitors have gone and they can just be quietly at home with their newborn child.

The fourteenth-century Swedish mystic St Bridget, in one of her visions, sees the Christ-child radiant with light and this is reflected in some of the art of the time, such as the nativity scene by Geertgen tot Sint Jans in the National Gallery in London, as it is here. In this radiant light, that of Joseph's lamp looks quite dim.

The setting, far from being a stable, is provided by two rather ornate classical pillars against a beautiful distant background. In the Renaissance depictions of this scene two details began to appear. One is of Mary kneeling on the ground before the child, hands closed in prayer. The other is of angels singing or playing on instruments. Here we see a lute and a flageolet.

NATIVITY
GB monogrammist (d. 1574)
Royal Collection

The visit of the shepherds

In that region there were shepherds living in the fields, keeping watch over their flock by night. Then an angel of the Lord stood before them, and the glory of the Lord shone around them, and they were terrified. But the angel said to them, 'Do not be afraid; for see—I am bringing you good news of great joy for all the people: to you is born this day in the city of David a Saviour, who is the Messiah, the Lord. This will be a sign for you: you will find a child wrapped in bands of cloth and lying in a manger.' And suddenly there was with the angel a multitude of the heavenly host, praising God and saying,

> 'Glory to God in the highest heaven, and
> on earth peace among those whom he favours!'

When the angels had left them and gone into heaven, the shepherds said to one another, 'Let us go now to Bethlehem and see this thing that has taken place, which the Lord has made known to us.' So they went with haste and found Mary and Joseph, and the child lying in the manger. When they saw this, they made known what had been told them about this child; and all who heard it were amazed at what the shepherds told them. But Mary treasured all these words and pondered them in her heart. The shepherds returned, glorifying and praising God for all they had heard and seen, as it had been told them.

From the Gospel of Luke, chapter 2

**THE ADORATION OF
THE SHEPHERDS**
Jacopo Bassano (1510–92)
King's drawing room,
Kensington Palace

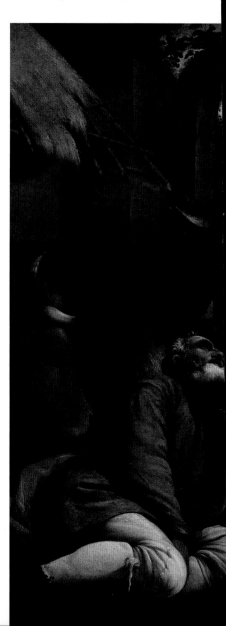

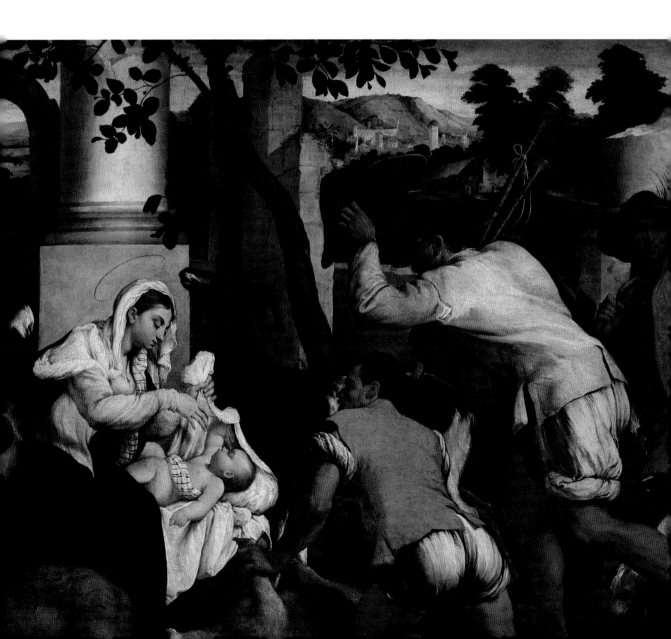

This is a very naturalistic scene. Mary pulls back the cloth so that the newborn babe can be seen and she looks down, all attention like any new mother. Joseph lies on the left, thoroughly relaxed; the shepherd kneeling down offers a trussed sheep, and to the bottom right dogs sniff about. The standing shepherd carries his bagpipes and lifts his hat with his left hand while the third shepherd is looking around. At the same time the scene is like a stage setting, with the spotlight on the mother and child but picking up the sheen of the shepherd's garments and Joseph's trousers. It is also full of symbolism. The familiar ox and ass from Isaiah 1.3, the empty Temple indicating the end of Judaism, and the ruined building to the right the end of Roman paganism. The light on the distant background suggests it is the dawn of a new age.

Bassano was born and worked in a village near Venice but was influenced by a range of artists from Venice itself. He was very popular for his genre paintings using the faces of local people and including animals. It was during this period that the visit of the shepherds began to be painted more frequently. Previously the nativity scenes had been dominated by the visit of the three kings. They did not lose their popularity but at the same time a desire to show more ordinary people, such as the shepherds, grew, a development that suited Bassano perfectly.

In 2006, Her Majesty the Queen reflected:

'I have lived long enough to know that things never remain quite the same for very long. One of the things that has not changed all that much for me is the celebration of Christmas. It remains a time when I try to put aside the anxieties of the moment and remember that Christ was born to bring peace and tolerance to a troubled world.

'The birth of Jesus naturally turns our thoughts to all newborn children and what the future holds for them. For Christians, Christmas marks the birth of our Saviour, but it is also a wonderful occasion to bring the generations together in a shared festival of peace, tolerance and goodwill.'

The visit of the kings

In the time of King Herod, after Jesus was born in Bethlehem of Judea, wise men from the East came to Jerusalem, asking, 'Where is the child who has been born king of the Jews? For we observed his star at its rising, and have come to pay him homage.' When King Herod heard this, he was frightened, and all Jerusalem with him; and calling together all the chief priests and scribes of the people, he inquired of them where the Messiah was to be born. They told him, 'In Bethlehem of Judea; for so it has been written by the prophet:

'And you, Bethlehem, in the land of Judah,
are by no means least among
the rulers of Judah;
for from you shall come a ruler
who is to shepherd my people Israel.'

Then Herod secretly called for the wise men and learned from them the exact time when the star had appeared. Then he sent them to Bethlehem, saying, 'Go and search diligently for the child; and when you have found him, bring me word so that I may also go and pay him homage.' When they had heard the king, they set out; and there, ahead of them, went the star that they had seen at its rising, until it stopped over the place where the child was. When they saw that the star had stopped, they were overwhelmed with joy. On entering the house, they saw the child with Mary his mother; and they knelt down and paid him homage. Then, opening their treasure-chests, they offered him gifts of gold, frankincense, and myrrh.

From the Gospel of Matthew, chapter 2

**THE ADORATION
OF THE KINGS**
Sebastiano Ricci (1659–1734)
Royal Collection

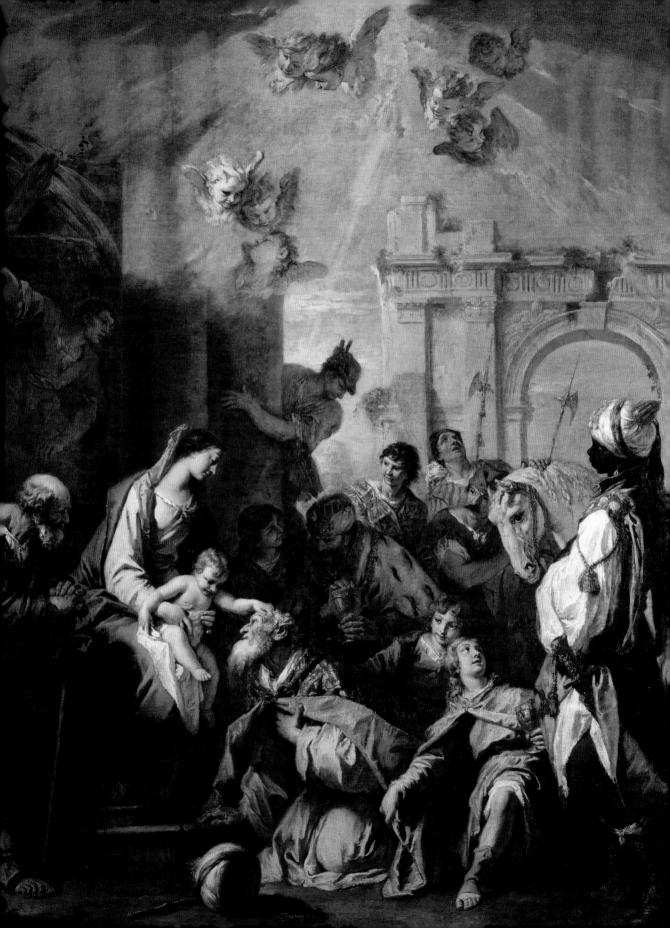

The visit of the three kings to worship the Christ-child gave rise to one of the richest developments in art. In the Roman catacombs three magi in Persian hats almost dance along like fire flies. In the great sixth-century mosaic in Sant'Apollinare Nuovo in Ravenna they are again in Persian hats but this time very richly attired. During the Middle Ages the magi became kings and began to be differentiated, one young, one middle aged and one old. A little later, one of them was depicted black, indicating not just all ages of humanity but all continents. During the Renaissance, artists vied with one another in depicting the size and wealth of the kings, sometimes showing their retinue trailing back miles over the hills.

In this depiction by Sebastiano Ricci the retinue is all crowded into a small space, as it were all coming close to get a good view. Mary is looking down adoringly at the Christ-child, while he holds his hand out to pat/bless the head on the aged king. Behind him a middle-aged king bends low and offers a gift. To the far right, a young black king stands with dignity. All around, children and adults and a white charger jostle. In the golden light above, angels also crowd in. Meanwhile, on the left, Joseph leans quietly on his stick and looks on. Once again the pillar suggests the Jewish Temple being displaced and the ruins the failure of the Roman world. To the far left can be seen the stable in which Christ, the bringer of a new world, is born.

Ricci painted in Venice during the late Baroque period, whose characteristics can be seen in this painting in the cherubs in a golden sky and the general exuberance.

In 1988, Her Majesty the Queen reflected:

'The star [of Bethlehem] has lit the way for
all of us ever since, and there should be no
one who feels shut out from that welcoming
and guiding light. The legends of Christmas
about the ox and the ass suggest that even the
animals are not outside that loving care.'

2
HOLY FAMILY

'Christmas commemorates the birth of a child, who was born to ordinary people, and who grew up very simply in his own small home town. The infant Jesus was fortunate in one very important respect. His parents were loving and considerate. They did their utmost to protect him from harm. They left their own home and became refugees, to save him from King Herod, and they brought him up according to the traditions of their faith.'

The Queen's Christmas broadcast, 1986

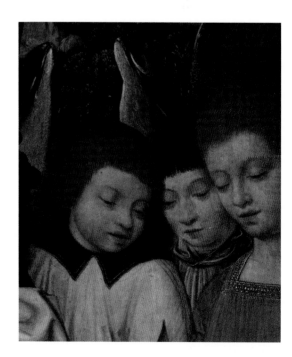

DETAIL FROM
**THE HOLY FAMILY
WITH ANGELS**
Follower of Joos van
Cleve (d. 1540/1)
Queen's private chapel,
Hampton Court Palace

The escape from Herod

Having been warned in a dream not to return to Herod, [the wise men] left for their own country by another road.

Now after they had left, an angel of the Lord appeared to Joseph in a dream and said, 'Get up, take the child and his mother, and flee to Egypt, and remain there until I tell you; for Herod is about to search for the child, to destroy him.' Then Joseph got up, took the child and his mother by night, and went to Egypt, and remained there until the death of Herod. This was to fulfil what had been spoken by the Lord through the prophet, 'Out of Egypt I have called my son.'

When Herod saw that he had been tricked by the wise men, he was infuriated, and he sent and killed all the children in and around Bethlehem who were two years old or under, according to the time that he had learned from the wise men. Then was fulfilled what had been spoken through the prophet Jeremiah:

'A voice was heard in Ramah,
wailing and loud lamentation,
Rachel weeping for her children;
she refused to be consoled, because they are
no more.'

When Herod died, an angel of the Lord suddenly appeared in a dream to Joseph in Egypt and said, 'Get up, take the child and his mother, and go to the land of Israel, for those who were seeking the child's life are dead.' Then Joseph got up, took the child and his mother, and went to the land of Israel. But when he heard that Archelaus was ruling over Judea in place of his father Herod, he was afraid to go there. And after being warned in a dream, he went away to the district of Galilee. There he made his home in a town called Nazareth, so that what had been spoken through the prophets might be fulfilled, 'He will be called a Nazorean.'

From the Gospel of Matthew, chapter 2

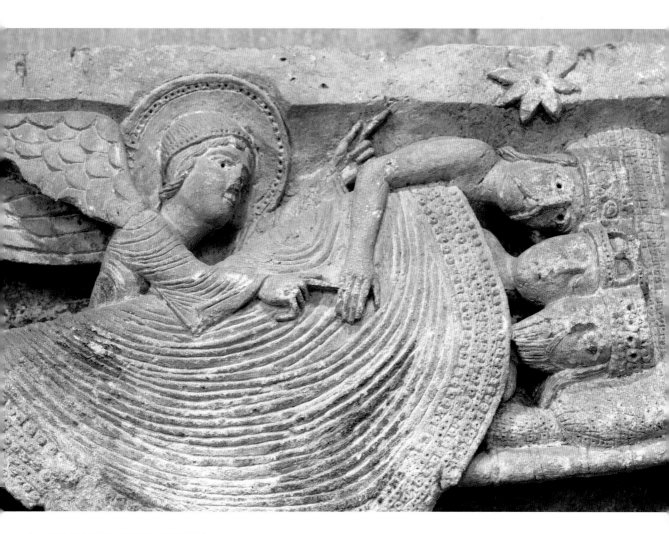

**AN ANGEL APPEARS TO THE
THREE KINGS IN A DREAM**
Gislebertus, active in Autun
Cathedral 1125–35
Autun Cathedral

This sculpture is famous not just for the quality
of the work but because it contains the words,
Gislebertus hoc fecit: 'Gislebertus made this.' The
vast armies of skilled craftsmen who produced
such outstanding work on churches and cathedrals
in the Middle Ages are for the most part
anonymous. They were part of teams working
for the glory of God. Gislebertus is the first one
whose name we know. It has been suggested that
this is the name of the patron not the sculptor, but
a patron would not have described his patronage
in those terms. Gislebertus did much work at
Cluny, at Vézelay and at Saint-Lazare, the
Cathedral of Autun. This is one of four capitals
based on the story of the wise men at Autun.

Here the three kings sleep in the same bed,
with their crowns on to highlight who they are.
The angel lightly touches the hand of one and
wakes him. With the other hand he points to
the star which will guide them safely home. The
whole movement of the angel is harmonious: the
folds in the blanket, the movement of the arms,
the nimbus and wings forming a circle. The
angel's face, despite a broken nose, is lovely. The
whole work is gentle and graceful, conveying the
message of divine grace.

The art of this period, Romanesque, had
a particular appeal to people in the twentieth
century, as in our own. Its symbolic approach
seemed to chime in well with modernism and its
swing away from any kind of literalism. This has
been particularly true in the field of religious art.

THE FLIGHT TO EGYPT
Giuseppe Bottani (1717–1884)
Royal Collection

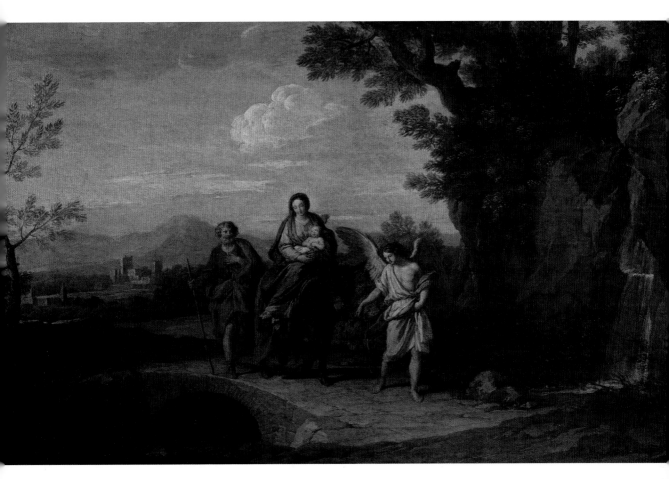

This scene was depicted in the fourth century but only became popular after the tenth. Many paintings drew not only on the Gospel account in Matthew recounted above, but on legends contained in the apocryphal Gospels. In this version by Bottani these have been excluded except for the inclusion of the waterfall on the right, which would have been natural to include anyway.

Bottani painted landscape in the tradition of Claude and Poussin and the theme of this painting encouraged him to make the most of his talent with this. There is a distant view of Jerusalem, situated not far from Bethlehem, from which the family are fleeing. In the distance there is a range of mountains set off by a striking sky. The family on the move is nicely framed by a solitary tree on the left and a dark thick one on the right as they are raised into the light as they cross over a well-made bridge. There is a sense of movement as the family emerges from the past into a dark unknown. But they have an angel to guide them, here pointing down to the ground as though to indicate an obstacle they need to avoid. Mary carries the Christ-child as she sits side-saddle on a donkey, and Joseph walks behind with his staff.

Mother, father and angels

When [Mary and Joseph] had finished everything required by the law of the Lord, they returned to Galilee, to their own town of Nazareth. The child grew and became strong, filled with wisdom; and the favour of God was upon him. **From the Gospel of Luke, chapter 2**

In the fifteenth century, Siena developed its own distinctive style of painting, which was different from that of Florence in a number of respects. It was characterized by rich, vibrant colours and a concern for detailed embellishment on a golden background. Southern Italy, after the fall of the Western empire, was part of the Byzantine empire, with its last outpost, Bari, falling in 1071. Something of the Byzantine influence can still be seen in the paintings of this period in their resemblance to earlier icons and their devotional feel. In this painting Mary looks to her right, as does the child Jesus. Two saints look on, possibly St Jerome to the left and St Bernadino of Siena on the right. Above them are six angels. Inscribed on the halo of Mary are the words *Ave, Gratia Plena Dominu[s tecum]*: 'Hail, full of grace, the Lord [is with thee].' The tooling of the work is sophisticated, with a wide variety of punches being used.

The difference with earlier icons can be seen in the fact that, instead of Mary pointing to Christ, often looking older, as the one to be followed,

the focus is on Jesus as a charming child. He has a slight smile and is holding a goldfinch in his hand. Goldfinches were very common in Italy in the fifteenth century and were often kept, tied to a string, as a pet. Although goldfinches are not mentioned in the Bible they have been found in 486 paintings, almost all in scenes of the Madonna. In the widest sense they symbolize the redemption and resurrection brought by Christ.

Sano di Pietro had a busy workshop in Siena, which produced numerous paintings, many of the same scene. He was also a respected member of the town establishment. His death notice read: *Pictor famosus et homo tous deditus Deo* ('A famous painter and a man wholly dedicated to God').

THE VIRGIN AND CHILD, TWO SAINTS AND SIX ANGELS
Sano di Pietro (1406–81)
Royal Collection

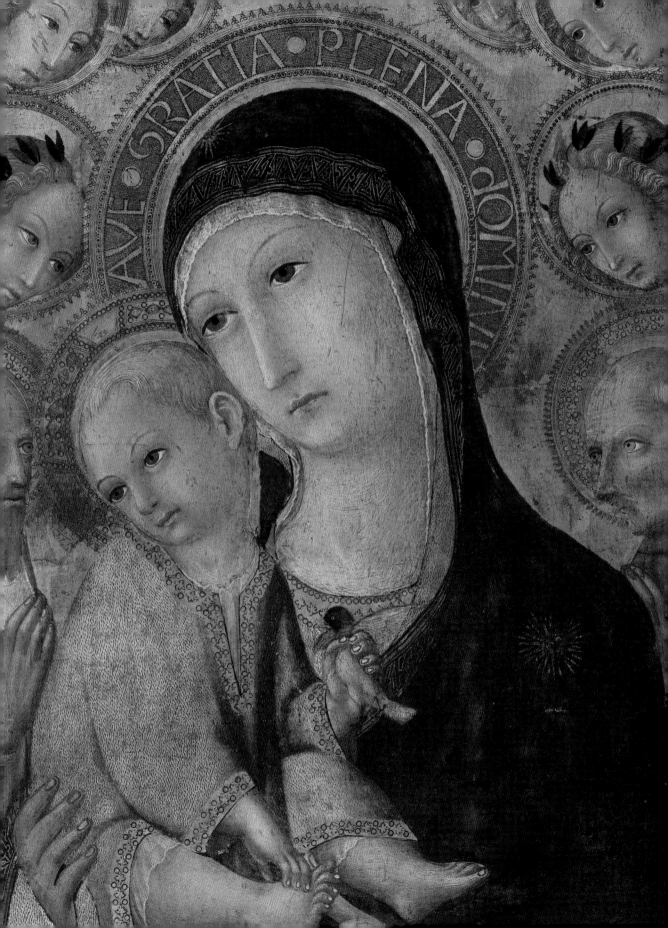

In art the biblical references to Joseph were supplemented by scenes from the apocryphal Gospels, which were later incorporated into *The Golden Legend,* a collection of hagiographies widely read in late medieval Europe. Joseph is not always treated sympathetically. But in the fourteenth and fifteenth centuries the holy family became a subject for devotion, and Joseph came into prominence in his own right. It is to this period that this painting belongs. The note on it in the Royal Collection states: 'The picture is of some quality and by a distinct hand. Attributed to Guido Reni in the eighteenth century, it is not related to him, but is closer in general to Maratta [Maratti], though not by him.'

The painting depicts Joseph and Jesus in an unusual pose, not facing the viewer but aslant, with a sad-looking Joseph gazing up at the cross. It is the child, healthy looking, even chubby, who dominates the picture both by his size and the mature, comforting look in his face as he holds the cross in one hand and supports the head of Joseph with the other. It is as though he is saying, 'Yes, the cross lies ahead but I will support you.'

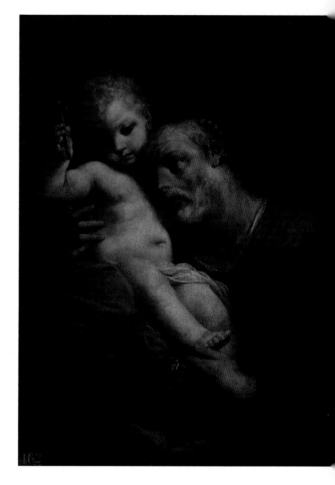

ST JOSEPH WITH THE INFANT CHRIST
Follower of Carlo Maratti (1625–1713)
Royal Collection

Joos van Cleve was a leading painter in Antwerp combining traditional Netherlandish techniques with influences from the Renaissance. He is known for his sensitivity to colour and unique solidarity of figures. He was one of the first to introduce broad landscapes into his figures. All these features are present in this painting. In the nineteenth century it was attributed to Quinten Massys, but because of the striking landscape in the background to this painting it is now thought to be by a follower of Joos van Cleve.

Mary is shown sitting on a throne, but one of wood not gold and bejewelled. She is nursing the Christ-child who is asleep. To the left, a balding Joseph looks down adoringly. In front of him is a metal dish containing grapes and other fruit. To the right, three angels are singing, one of them

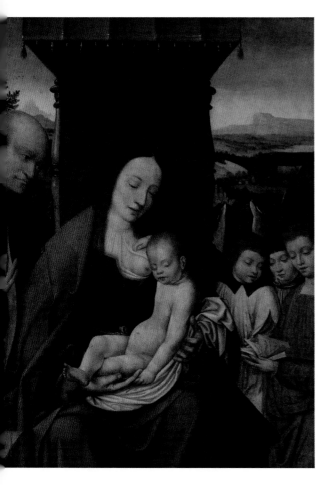

THE HOLY FAMILY WITH ANGELS
Follower of Joos van Cleve (d. 1540/1)
Queen's private chapel,
Hampton Court Palace

with a book of music. Behind this intimate scene
is a broad, deep landscape with haunting shades
of colour. A sense of serenity pervades the scene
with Mary who, eyes half closed, is seemingly
caught up in the music.

In 2006, Her Majesty Queen Elizabeth reflected:

'The wisdom and experience of
the great religions point to the
need to nurture and guide the
young, and to encourage respect
for the elderly. Christ himself told
his disciples to let the children
come to him, and Saint Paul
reminded parents to be gentle
with their children, and children
to appreciate their parents.

'We could use some of that
sturdy confidence and devastating
honesty with which children
rescue us from self-doubts and
self-delusions. We could borrow
that unstinting trust of the child
in its parents for our dealings with
each other.'

Growing in wisdom

Now every year his parents went to Jerusalem for the festival of the Passover. And when he was twelve years old, they went up as usual for the festival. When the festival was ended and they started to return, the boy Jesus stayed behind in Jerusalem, but his parents did not know it. Assuming that he was in the group of travellers, they went a day's journey. Then they started to look for him among their relatives and friends. When they did not find him, they returned to Jerusalem to search for him. After three days they found him in the temple, sitting among the teachers, listening to them and asking them questions. And all who heard him were amazed at his understanding and his answers. When his parents saw him they were astonished; and his mother said to him, 'Child, why have you treated us like this? Look, your father and I have been searching for you in great anxiety.' He said to them, 'Why were you searching for me? Did you not know that I must be in my Father's house?' But they did not understand what he said to them. Then he went down with them and came to Nazareth, and was obedient to them. His mother treasured all these things in her heart.

And Jesus increased in wisdom and in years, and in divine and human favour.

From the Gospel of Luke, chapter 2

Dürer was born in Nuremberg and his woodcuts quickly made him famous across Europe. Many of these have a strongly Gothic quality. But he was much influenced by the painters of the Italian Renaissance and produced a huge number of works in a variety of media which reflect this. This painting is one of them. Painted in Venice, in five days as he recorded, it is striking in the stark contrast it depicts between the hard, aged heads of the men and the innocence and beauty of the boy Jesus. This is accentuated by the way Jesus is set in a crowded circle of the heads of the doctors and by the varying shades of brown, orange and yellow which give his whiter face and blue/green robe prominence. Hands play a large role in the painting, the ones of the doctors tightly gripping the books they are expounding or gesticulating. While the two lower faces have dignity, the others are something of a caricature in their hostility, one of them very short of teeth. The one on the bottom left has an inscription on his head.

CHRIST AMONG THE DOCTORS
Albrecht Dürer (1471 – 1528)
Thyssen-Bornemisza
Museum, Madrid

In 2016, Her Majesty the Queen reflected:

'Jesus Christ lived obscurely for most of his life, and never travelled far. He was maligned and rejected by many, though he had done no wrong. And yet, billions of people now follow his teaching and find in him the guiding light for their lives. I am one of them because Christ's example helps me see the value of doing small things with great love, whoever does them and whatever they themselves believe.'

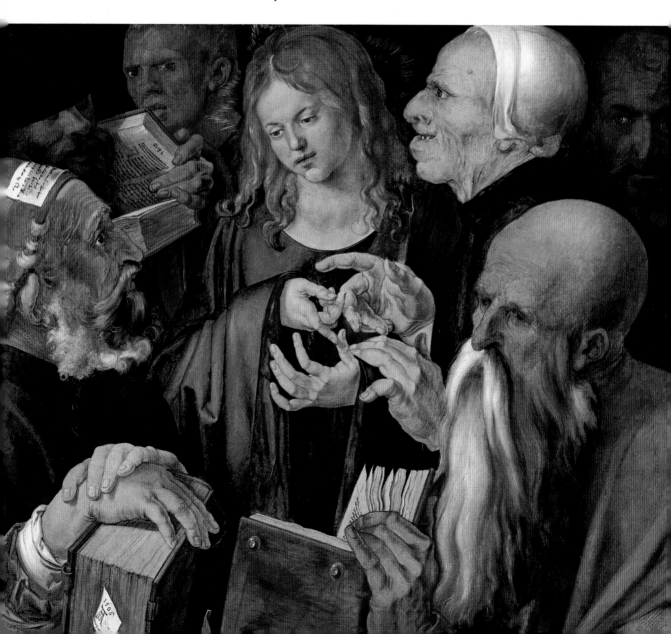

John Everett Millais was a founder member of
the Pre-Raphaelite brotherhood which sought
to recover realism in painting as opposed to the
idealization of Raphael and his followers. So this
painting shows a carpenter's shop in everyday
detail, its figures based on people known by the
artist. When first shown, it aroused huge hostility.

The Times described the painting as 'revolting'
and objected to the way in which the artist had
dared to depict the holy family as ordinary,
lowly people in a humble carpenter's shop
'with no conceivable omission of misery, of
dirt, of even disease, all finished with the same
loathsome minuteness'. Charles Dickens attacked
it no less fiercely but the result was to give the
Pre-Raphaelites prominence for the first time.

The painting is steeped in religious symbolism.
Jesus has cut his hand and blood drops on his
foot. Joseph holds the hand and Mary kneels on
the floor to comfort her son. His cousin, later
known as John the Baptist, brings a bowl of
water. In the background can be seen a ladder,
Jacob's ladder, linking heaven and earth, and
a carpenter's triangle symbolizing the Trinity.
A dove, symbol of the Holy Spirit, sits on
the ladder. Also in the background are sheep
indicating the flock of the Church Christ would
pastor, while on the table they are making a door,
for he will be the door that leads to eternal life.
Also on the table are some nails, while Mary's
mother, Anna, puts forward a pair of pincers.

**CHRIST IN THE HOUSE
OF HIS PARENTS ('THE
CARPENTER'S SHOP')**
John Millais (1829–96)
Tate Britain

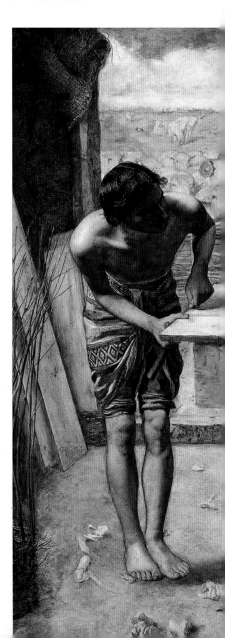

He came to his home town and . . . the people
said, '. . . Is not this the carpenter's son? Is not
his mother called Mary? And are not his brothers
James and Joseph and Simon and Judas?
From the Gospel of Matthew, chapter 13

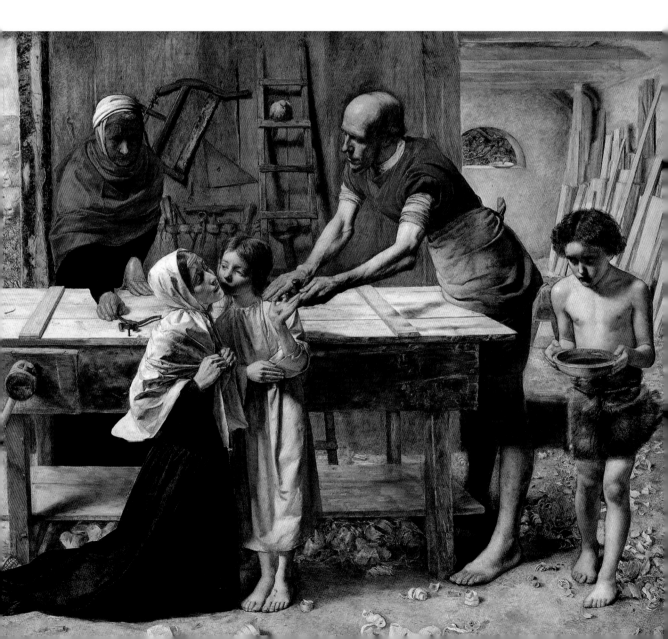

3
HEALER AND TEACHER

'When, as the Bible says, Christ grew in wisdom and understanding, he began his task of explaining and teaching just what it is that God wants from us. The two lessons that he had for us, which he underlined in everything he said and did, are the messages of God's love and how essential it is that we, too, should love other people.'

The Queen's Christmas broadcast, 1986

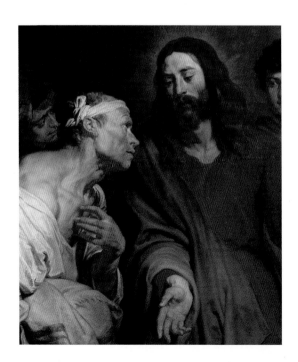

Jesus is baptized

In those days Jesus came from Nazareth of
Galilee and was baptized by John in the Jordan.
And just as he was coming up out of the water,
he saw the heavens torn apart and the Spirit
descending like a dove on him. And a voice came
from heaven, 'You are my Son, the Beloved; with
you I am well pleased.'
From the Gospel of Mark, chapter 1

THE BAPTISM OF CHRIST
Francesco Francia (1450–1517)
Royal Collection

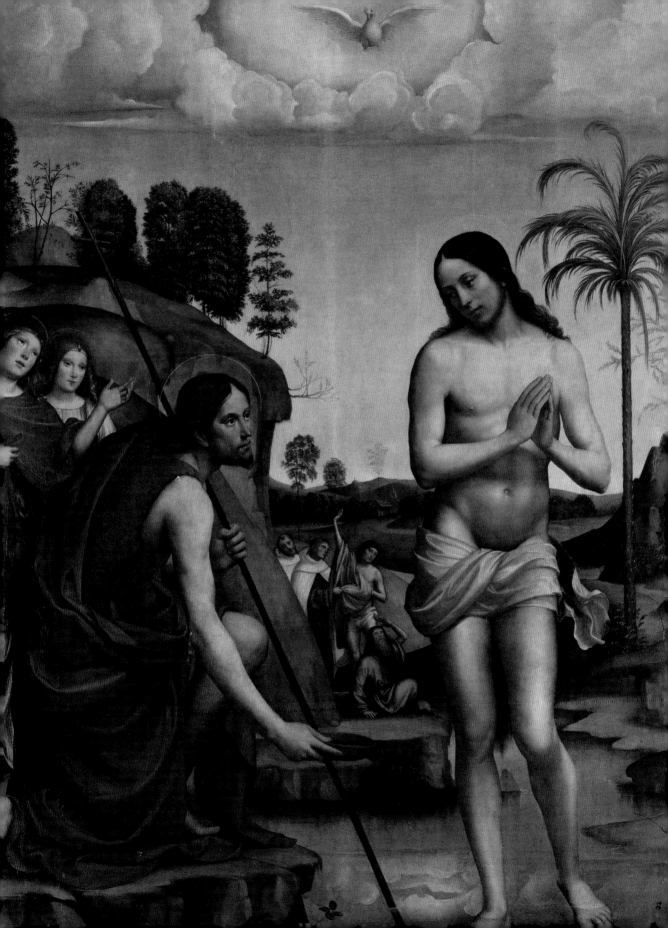

Francesco Francia, a goldsmith as well as a painter, lived in Bologna, where he had a large workshop. Although well thought of at the time, he was later overshadowed by artists of the High Renaissance, but his work, influenced by Raphael and Perugino, has its own quiet charm. We can see this if we contrast his version of the scene with the more famous one by Piero della Francesca in the National Gallery, which was painted not long before. That one is beautiful in its sheer strangeness. The one here by Francesco Francia is lovely in its sense of calm devotion. Both, however, adhere to classical notions of proportion and symmetry with verticals and horizontals being intersected by lines of different but matching angles. For example, the line of the rock face, the raised arm of a man undressing and John's rod stand in contrast to the pointing hands of the angels behind and the praying hands of Jesus.

Jesus, dressed only in a blue loincloth, stands in very shallow water. John kneels down to scoop out some water into a bowl to pour it over his head, as today a priest might use a scallop shell to baptize an infant at the font. The fact that John is kneeling brings to mind his saying that he is not worthy to untie the straps of Jesus' sandals.

In the background a group of people take off their clothes ready to be baptized. Above, in the clouds, a dove, symbolizing the Holy Spirit, hovers.

The Christian movement in history began when John the Baptist called people to turn away from their folly and look to God and his kingdom. Jesus responded to this call and as he was being baptized he learned of his own unique vocation. 'You are my Son, the Beloved.' He lived out the whole of his life as this Son to the one he addressed as 'Abba, Father', inspired by the Holy Spirit within him. The rod carried by John ends in a cross, an ominous reminder from the first as to what this vocation would entail.

There is a profound mystery about how Jesus thought of himself and his role but Sister Wendy Beckett, who lived a life of prayer as a hermit and became famous for her insights into art, makes a suggestive parallel when she writes:

> We can have some idea of what makes a person tick if they have an overriding preoccupation. An artist like Matisse, a musician like Mozart: one can imagine what was always present to them because their life revolved round it. There was no Matisse without art, Mozart's identity was his music. So I thought with Our Blessed Lord; the one absolute certainty we have about Him is His love for the Father. His awareness of the Father must have filled his mind from the earliest.[1]

This awareness was overwhelmingly confirmed in the words that Jesus heard at his baptism, words that warmed and strengthened him throughout his whole life and in death, which he met with an act of trust: 'Father, into thy hands I commend my spirit' (AV).

---

1 Sister Wendy Beckett and Robert Ellsberg, *Dearest Sister Wendy . . . A Surprising Story of Faith and Friendship* (Maryknoll, NY: Orbis Books, 2022), p. 174.

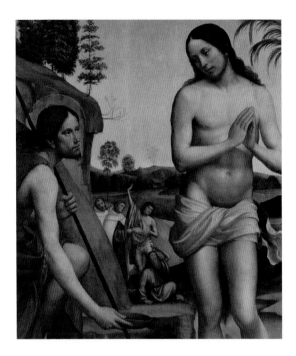

Jesus, dressed only in a blue loincloth, stands in very shallow water. John kneels down to scoop out some water into a bowl to pour it over his head, as today a priest might use a scallop shell to baptize an infant at the font. The fact that John is kneeling brings to mind his saying that he is not worthy to untie the straps of Jesus' sandals.

Jesus is tempted in the wilderness

Then Jesus was led up by the Spirit into the wilderness to be tempted by the devil. He fasted for forty days and forty nights, and afterwards he was famished. The tempter came and said to him, 'If you are the Son of God, command these stones to become loaves of bread.' But he answered, 'It is written,

> "One does not live by bread alone,
> but by every word that comes from the
> mouth of God."'

Then the devil took him to the holy city and placed him on the pinnacle of the temple, saying to him, 'If you are the Son of God, throw yourself down; for it is written,

> "He will command his angels concerning you",
> and "On their hands they will bear you up,
> so that you will not dash your foot
> against a stone."'

Jesus said to him, 'Again it is written, "Do not put the Lord your God to the test."'

Again, the devil took him to a very high mountain and showed him all the kingdoms of the world and their splendour; and he said to him, 'All these I will give you, if you will fall down and worship me.' Jesus said to him, 'Away with you, Satan! for it is written,

> "Worship the Lord your God,
> and serve only him."'

Then the devil left him, and suddenly angels came and waited on him.

From the Gospel of Matthew, chapter 4

TEMPTATION IN THE WILDERNESS
Briton Rivière (1840–1920)
Guildhall Art Gallery

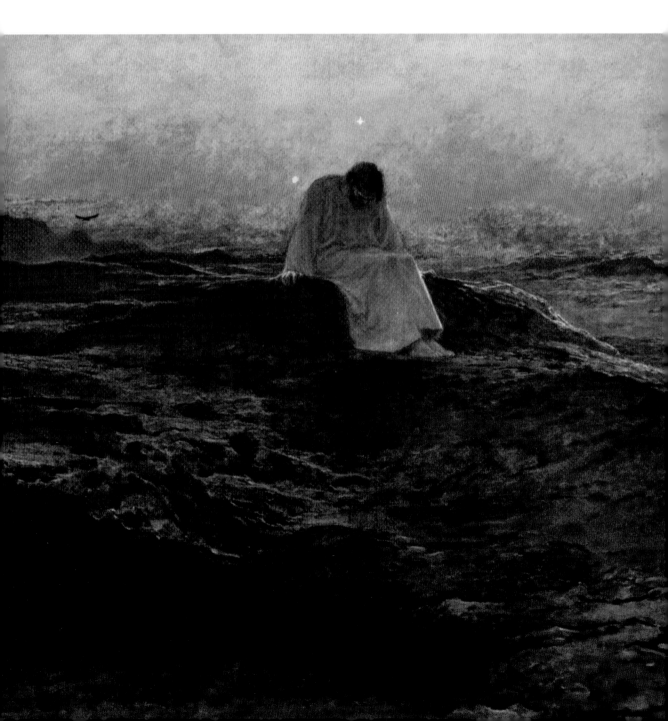

Traditional depictions of this scene show the devil, usually with horns, tempting Jesus. Here, however, there is no figure except Jesus, with his head bowed. The temptation is going on in his mind. Briton Rivière, a British artist of Huguenot descent, straddled the period of traditional Victorian art, through impressionism to modernism. In this painting we can see influences of all three. On the one hand it is traditionally figurative, a person in a landscape. On the other hand the landscape is clearly designed to create an emotion in the minds of the viewers.

The dark barrenness of the rocks contrasts with the lurid orange and red of the sky, and this indicates something of the crisis that is going on in the mind of Jesus, who is deeply immersed in his inner struggle. He had just heard the words, 'You are my beloved son.' He knew he had been given great, unusual powers. How was he to use those powers? Besides, was he really the Son of God? So he hears the insidious words, '*If* you are the Son of God'. He is invited to test out their reality. He is starving. He could turn those white rocks, shimmering in the sun, into loaves of bread. He could prove to others he was the Son of God by performing a great stunt like throwing himself off the pinnacle of the Temple and letting the angels sweep down to hold him up and break his fall. He could be an imperial dictator with the whole world at his command and turn it into God's kingdom. Each time he says, 'No. That is not the way.' The way he has to go will involve suffering, but meanwhile the angels come and strengthen him. It is in the mind that the great battles of life have to be fought. This is where we are tested.

In 2013, Her Majesty Queen Elizabeth reflected:

'We all need to get the balance right between action and reflection. With so many distractions, it is easy to forget to pause and take stock. Be it through contemplation, prayer, or even keeping a diary, many have found the practice of quiet personal reflection surprisingly rewarding, even discovering greater spiritual depth to their lives.'

Jesus calls his first disciples

As Jesus passed along the Sea of Galilee, he saw
Simon and his brother Andrew casting a net into
the lake—for they were fishermen. And Jesus said
to them, 'Follow me and I will make you fish for
people.' And immediately they left their nets and
followed him.

From the Gospel of Mark, chapter 1

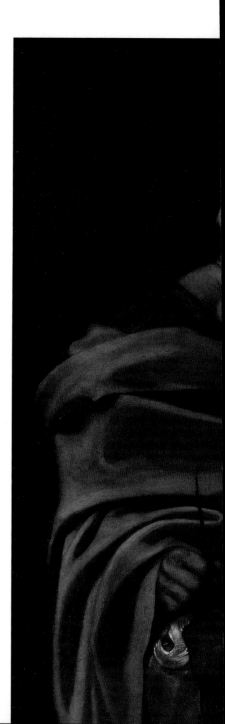

THE CALLING OF SAINTS
PETER AND ANDREW
Caravaggio (1571 – 1610)
Cumberland bedchamber,
Hampton Court Palace

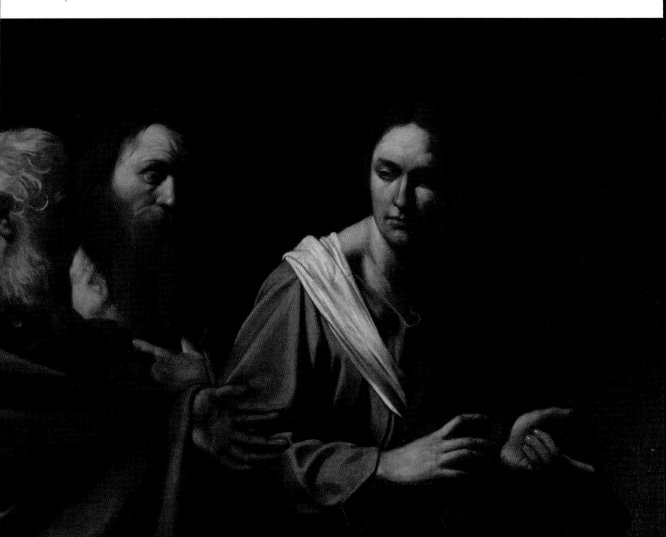

This is one of Caravaggio's most beautiful paintings. His characteristic contrast of light and dark is present, as is his sense of drama, but it is all in a gentler mode. This is partly achieved by the subdued gentle colours, the brown of Peter's handsome cloak and the gingery brown of Andrew's beard contrasting with the soft purple of Jesus' shirt and green of his cloak

The light picks up what Caravaggio wants us to focus on, the hands of the three figures and then their faces. The hands of Jesus, slender and elegant, point forward, where he wants Peter and Andrew to follow. One hand of Peter is holding a fish, while the other, a strong fisherman's hand, is open in surprise as though questioning, 'You really mean drop everything and just follow you?' The hand of Andrew points at himself, again with a sense of surprise, 'You mean me, you really mean me?' The face of Jesus, beardless and feminine, turns to look back at the two startled faces of the fishermen, both much older figures, half balding and heavily bearded, Peter traditionally depicted with his white hair.

Jesus, with his shapely neck and white sash, has a spiritual allure so strong that, despite their astonishment, they do leave their nets and follow him.

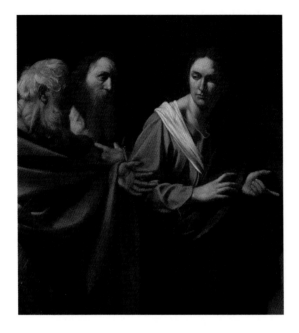

The light picks up what Caravaggio wants
us to focus on, the hands of the three figures
and then their faces. The hands of Jesus,
slender and elegant, point forward, where
he wants Peter and Andrew to follow.

An amazing catch

Once while Jesus was standing beside the lake of
Gennesaret, and the crowd was pressing in on
him to hear the word of God, he saw two boats
there at the shore of the lake; the fishermen had
gone out of them and were washing their nets.
He got into one of the boats, the one belonging
to Simon, and asked him to put out a little way
from the shore. Then he sat down and taught
the crowds from the boat. When he had finished
speaking, he said to Simon, 'Put out into the
deep water and let down your nets for a catch.'
Simon answered, 'Master, we have worked all
night long but have caught nothing. Yet if you
say so, I will let down the nets.' When they had
done this, they caught so many fish that their
nets were beginning to break. So they signalled
to their partners in the other boat to come and
help them. And they came and filled both boats,
so that they began to sink. But when Simon Peter
saw it, he fell down at Jesus' knees, saying, 'Go
away from me, Lord, for I am a sinful man!' For
he and all who were with him were amazed at
the catch of fish that they had taken; and so also
were James and John, sons of Zebedee, who were
partners with Simon. Then Jesus said to Simon,
'Do not be afraid; from now on you will be
catching people.'

From the Gospel of Luke, chapter 5

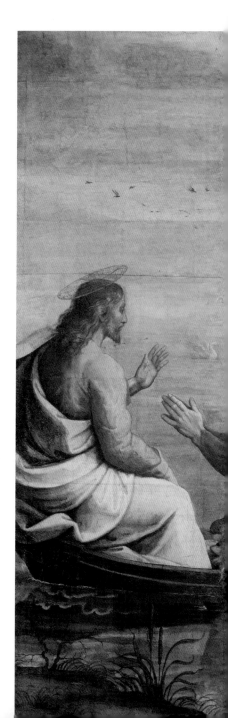

THE MIRACULOUS
DRAFT OF FISHES
Raphael (1483–1520)
Royal Collection on loan to the
Victoria and Albert Museum

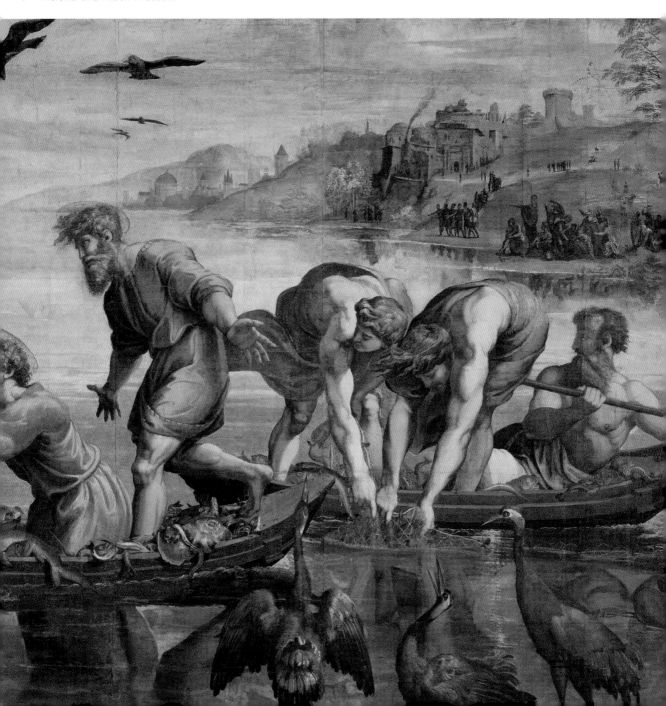

Jesus did many things and said many things that are not recorded in the Gospels. So it is always worth asking why some incidents were remembered and then written down. Clearly one reason this story was remembered was because miracles are by definition very rare and startling. But it was more than this: it was because a miracle in some way expressed the mind of Christ that it was included in a Gospel account. Behind this account is the knowledge that Christians were charged with preaching good news to all the world. They were to become fishers of people. But they also knew from their own experience what a daunting task this was, how their own human resources always seemed so inadequate. This story would have given them hope. When they seemed to fail, if they obeyed the Lord and put out once more, they would be abundantly blessed.

Raphael depicts that moment of abundance. One boat is filled to overflowing with fish, while in the other the disciples labour to pull up another heavy net. Meanwhile cormorants stand by to get their pickings and birds overhead fly in for their share.

Jesus sits from where he liked to teach, in the prow of the boat. Peter, with outstretched hands, feels overwhelmed by a sense of the holiness of Jesus and his own unworthiness. While the figures in the painting are depicted in a straightforward but harmonious way, the shades of blue on the lake and in the sky suggest that something more is going on than meets the eye.

Galilee even today is a calm, low-lying and undeveloped spot, but Raphael has clearly depicted something more like the Italian lakes, with buildings and hills around. This is a cartoon, a preliminary study for a tapestry for the Sistine Chapel, commissioned by Pope Leo X.

In 2000, Her Majesty Queen Elizabeth reflected:

'To many of us our beliefs are of fundamental importance. For me the teachings of Christ and my own personal accountability before God provide a framework in which I try to lead my life.

'I believe that the Christian message, in the words of a familiar blessing, remains profoundly important to us all:

"Go forth into the world in peace, be of good courage, hold fast that which is good, render to no man evil for evil, strengthen the faint-hearted, support the weak, help the afflicted, honour all men."

'It is a simple message of compassion and yet as powerful as ever today, two thousand years after Christ's birth.'

Jesus has pity on the sick

And just then some people were carrying a paralysed man lying on a bed. When Jesus saw their faith, he said to the paralytic, 'Take heart, son; your sins are forgiven.' Then some of the scribes said to themselves, 'This man is blaspheming.' But Jesus, perceiving their thoughts, said, 'Why do you think evil in your hearts? For which is easier, to say, "Your sins are forgiven", or to say, "Stand up and walk"? But so that you may know that the Son of Man has authority on earth to forgive sins'—he then said to the paralytic—'Stand up, take your bed and go to your home.' And he stood up and went to his home. When the crowds saw it, they were filled with awe, and they glorified God, who had given such authority to human beings.

From the Gospel of Matthew, chapter 9

This was painted by van Dyck when he was only 20 and working in the studio of Rubens, who may have provided the outline and guided him. The jostling half-length figures and the mixture of classical and down-to-earth faces reflect the influence of Caravaggio.

The paralysed man is based on an antique statue thought to be of the death of Seneca, of which Rubens made some sketches. The wretched state of this man stands in contrast to the handsome classical poses of Jesus and the Apostle, perhaps James. This Apostle is watching the reaction of the paralysed man while a man behind the paralytic stares expectantly at Jesus. The whole scene conveys a sense of something momentous about to happen, something that will take the paralysed man into the glorious light and freedom of the countryside on the right, as both his body and his spirit are healed.

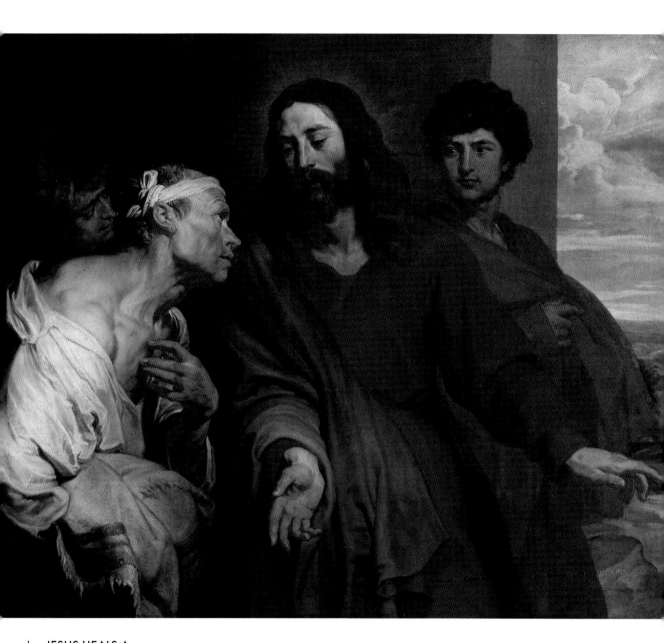

**JESUS HEALS A
PARALYSED MAN**
Anthony van Dyck (1599–1641)
Royal Collection

Now there was a woman who had been suffering from haemorrhages for twelve years; and though she had spent all she had on physicians, no one could cure her. She came up behind him and touched the fringe of his clothes, and immediately her haemorrhage stopped. Then Jesus asked, 'Who touched me?' When all denied it, Peter said, 'Master, the crowds surround you and press in on you.' But Jesus said, 'Someone touched me; for I noticed that power had gone out from me.' When the woman saw that she could not remain hidden, she came trembling; and falling down before him, she declared in the presence of all the people why she had touched him, and how she had been immediately healed. He said to her, 'Daughter, your faith has made you well; go in peace.'

From the Gospel of Luke, chapter 8

Some of the earliest Christian art was carved on the sides of coffins. Many Roman sarcophagi are magnificent and those Christians who could afford it from the third century onwards used their own burial as an opportunity to display their Christian faith. So, instead of the usual pagan scenes, they carved incidents from the life of Christ.

This sarcophagus is very Roman in style, with its columns and capitals and motif of putti with their bunches of grapes. The figures could pass for Roman senators in their flowing robes and dignified unshaven heads. This is how many Christians pictured Christ at the time, not as a bearded older man, as later became the norm, but youthful with a smooth face.

The significance of the incident is found not in the towering figures but in the kneeling, diminutive woman touching the hem of Christ's robe.

As she touched Jesus he knew some power had flowed from him. When Peter, shown here very close to Christ, pointed out that the crowd was pressing on him from all around and it could have been anyone, the woman came forward and Jesus affirmed her faith. In the carving, Christ is shown both blessing and protecting her, sheltering her with his outstretched arm and hand. I remember as a young student talking to a close friend of mine who suddenly said that he found this incident the most moving of all the stories in the Gospels.

In 1999, Her Majesty Queen Elizabeth reflected:

'At the centre of our lives – today and tomorrow – must be the message of caring for others, the message at the heart of Christianity and of all the great religions.

'This message – love your neighbour as yourself – may be over 2,000 years old. But it is as relevant today as it ever was.'

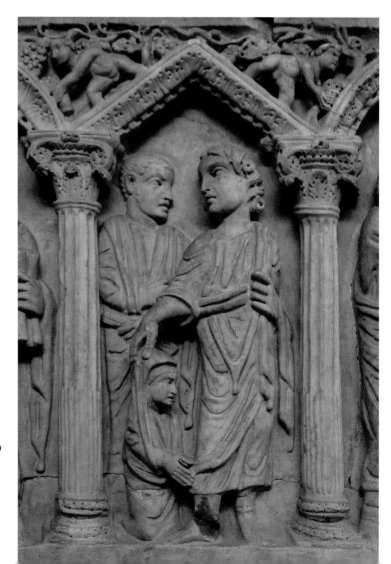

THE WOMAN WHO COULD NOT STOP BLEEDING
Detail from an early fourth-century sarcophagus
The Vatican Museum

Jesus calls an outsider

As Jesus was walking along, he saw a man called Matthew sitting at the tax booth; and he said to him, 'Follow me.' And he got up and followed him.

From the Gospel of Matthew, chapter 9

**THE CALLING OF
ST MATTHEW**
Caravaggio (1571 – 1610)
San Luigi dei Francesi, Rome

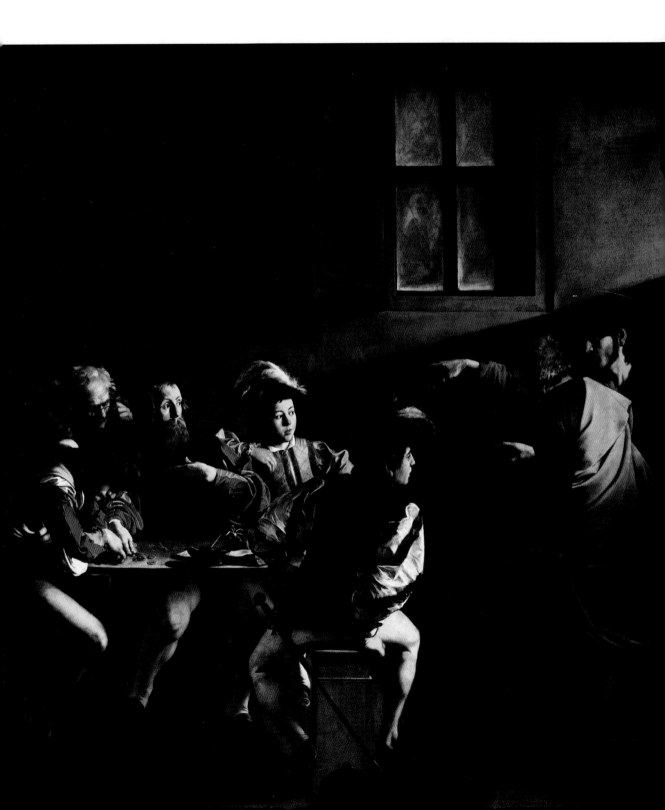

The first impact this painting makes on the viewer is the strong contrast between the dark and the light, a feature of so many of Caravaggio's paintings. The bottom two-thirds of the painting and the left-hand half are mostly black. The light on the wall is subdued because the artist wants our eyes to be drawn to the details that the light picks out. Here the eye moves horizontally right to left and back again. On the right, half-hidden, is the face of Christ, lean and authoritative. Christ is mostly hidden – by Peter – because the focus is on his arm and hand pointing. Round the table the four characters all respond differently. The man furthest to the right turns with a somewhat bovine look on his face. The pretty young man, beautifully dressed, turns with a half-amused, sceptical expression. Matthew, middle aged and bearded, points to himself. 'You mean me? Do you really mean me?' On the far left the man gazes down at the table, fingering the money. Very intriguing is the man next to him looking thoughtful, wondering what to make of it, caught between the desire for money and the call of Christ. He has not yet made up his mind.

You feel that Caravaggio enjoyed painting this scene, with its varied reactions of the characters in it and the down-to-earth details, the solid table, the muscular legs of the men, the sword prominently displayed.

The Gospel narrative is stark in the extreme, just the call and the immediate response. We learn nothing of what, if anything, preceded the call. We do know something of what happened after. For in the list of 12 Apostles the only one with his occupation mentioned is 'Matthew the tax collector', as we might refer to 'John the artist' or 'Bill the soldier' even if they were retired. Tax collectors were doubly unpopular at the time. They collaborated with the occupying regime, and they were known to increase their own earnings at the expense of those from whom they were gathering tax. But Jesus made a point of both eating with outsiders and calling them to follow him. Caravaggio well conveys the surprise and drama of the scene.

In 2007, Her Majesty Queen Elizabeth reflected:

'Throughout his ministry, Jesus of Nazareth reached out and made friends with people whom others ignored or despised. It was in this way that he proclaimed his belief that, in the end, we are all brothers and sisters in one human family.'

A venture of faith

Immediately he made the disciples get into the boat and go on ahead to the other side, while he dismissed the crowds. And after he had dismissed the crowds, he went up the mountain by himself to pray. When evening came, he was there alone, but by this time the boat, battered by the waves, was far from the land, for the wind was against them. And early in the morning he came walking towards them on the lake. But when the disciples saw him walking on the lake, they were terrified, saying, 'It is a ghost!' And they cried out in fear. But immediately Jesus spoke to them and said, 'Take heart, it is I; do not be afraid.'

Peter answered him, 'Lord, if it is you, command me to come to you on the water.' He said, 'Come.' So Peter got out of the boat, started walking on the water, and came towards Jesus. But when he noticed the strong wind, he became frightened, and beginning to sink, he cried out, 'Lord, save me!' Jesus immediately reached out his hand and caught him, saying to him, 'You of little faith, why did you doubt?' When they got into the boat, the wind ceased. And those in the boat worshipped him, saying, 'Truly you are the Son of God.'

From the Gospel of Matthew, chapter 14

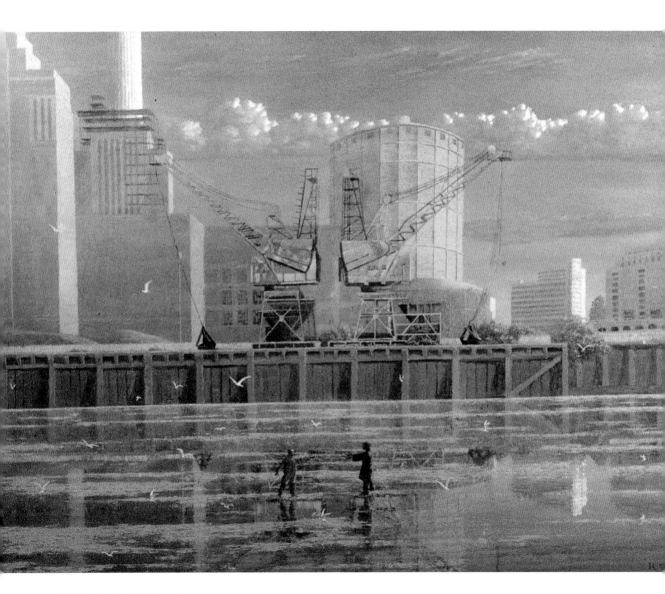

WALKING ON WATER III
Roger Wagner (b. 1957)
Private collection

This painting by Roger Wagner depicts Battersea
Power Station before it was turned into flats, with
large cranes standing before it on the bank of the
Thames. On the river, Christ in blue holds out
both hands welcoming Peter, who holds out one
hand calling for help.

In one sense Wagner is an old-fashioned
painter, with a meticulous attention to detail.
He can take a year over a painting. At the same
time he is a modernist in the sense that T. S.
Eliot was, depicting the modern world but in
a way that draws on the depths of tradition.
He is not an archaeological painter, trying to
image biblical scenes as they might have been,
say like Mantegna. Rather he wants to show the
modern world made strange by being suffused
with biblical light. He wants to show an everyday
scene but with something other going on. So it is
that this painting, with its mixture of blues, has a
haunting, surreal quality.

Wagner is an accomplished poet and in a
poem on this painting he makes it clear that it is
not so much about what is reported in the New
Testament as it is about the venture of faith.[2]

2   Richard Harries, *The Image of Christ in Modern Art*,
Farnham: Ashgate, 2013, p. 149.

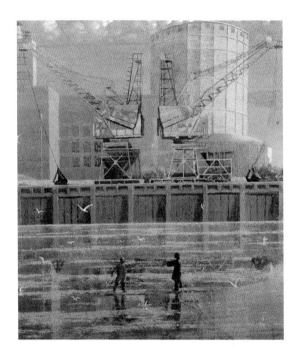

This painting by Roger Wagner depicts Battersea Power Station before it was turned into flats, with large cranes standing before it on the bank of the Thames. On the river, Christ in blue holds out both hands welcoming Peter, who holds out one hand calling for help.

The good Samaritan

Just then a lawyer stood up to test Jesus. 'Teacher,' he said, 'what must I do to inherit eternal life?' He said to him, 'What is written in the law? What do you read there?' He answered, 'You shall love the Lord your God with all your heart, and with all your soul, and with all your strength, and with all your mind; and your neighbour as yourself.' And he said to him, 'You have given the right answer; do this, and you will live.'

But wanting to justify himself, he asked Jesus, 'And who is my neighbour?' Jesus replied, 'A man was going down from Jerusalem to Jericho, and fell into the hands of robbers, who stripped him, beat him, and went away, leaving him half dead. Now by chance a priest was going down that road; and when he saw him, he passed by on the other side. So likewise a Levite, when he came to the place and saw him, passed by on the other side. But a Samaritan while travelling came near him; and when he saw him, he was moved with pity. He went to him and bandaged his wounds, having poured oil and wine on them. Then he put him on his own animal, brought him to an inn, and took care of him. The next day he took out two denarii, gave them to the innkeeper, and said, "Take care of him; and when I come back, I will repay you whatever more you spend." Which of these three, do you think, was a neighbour to the man who fell into the hands of the robbers?'

He said, 'The one who showed him mercy.' Jesus said to him, 'Go and do likewise.' **From the Gospel of Luke, chapter 10**

THE GOOD SAMARITAN
Rembrandt (1606–69)
The Wallace Collection, London

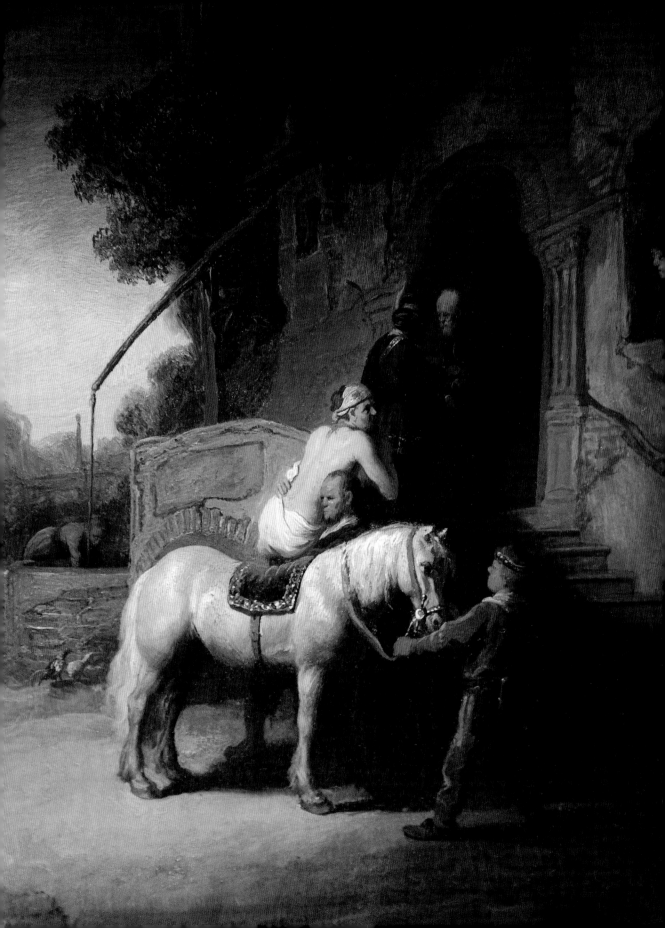

This is a quiet, everyday scene. There are many
times and places where it might have taken
place. A servant holds the horse, another one
lifts a half-naked man off it, while at the doorway
a man negotiates with the innkeeper. Behind
the house, to one side, a woman gets on with
drawing water from the well. In his poem 'Musée
des Beaux Arts', W. H. Auden describes how
the world goes on its way even as someone is
suffering. So we could say about this painting,
everyone goes about their everyday jobs while
someone is carrying out a good deed. There is
nothing spectacular or dramatic about the scene,
yet in its quietness and ordinariness there is
something truly good going on. A man, obviously
of some substance as we can see from the horse
with its fine covering, is making sure that the
injured traveller is well cared for at the inn and
that the innkeeper has more than enough to
cover the expenses of his care.

   Rembrandt was attracted to this scene and
sketched or painted it a number of times.
This is thought to be an early version.
Somewhat puzzling is the fact that the
house is built half out of a Roman ruin,
as we can see from the surviving pillars by
the door and the Roman brickwork by the
stairs. Perhaps he wanted to suggest a new
order of charity or altruistic care arising out
of the ruins of the old self-seeking world.

In 2004, Her Majesty Queen Elizabeth reflected:

'For me one of the most important of Christ's teachings is contained in the parable of the good Samaritan, when Jesus answers the question, 'Who is my neighbour?' It is a timeless story of a victim of a mugging who was ignored by his own countrymen but helped by a foreigner – and a despised foreigner at that.

   'The implication drawn by Jesus is clear. Everyone is our neighbour, no matter what race, creed or colour. The need to look after a fellow human being is far more important than any cultural or religious differences.'

The mote and the beam

'Do not judge, so that you may not be judged. For with the judgement you make you will be judged, and the measure you give will be the measure you get. Why do you see the speck in your neighbour's eye, but do not notice the log in your own eye? Or how can you say to your neighbour, "Let me take the speck out of your eye", while the log is in your own eye? You hypocrite, first take the log out of your own eye, and then you will see clearly to take the speck out of your neighbour's eye.'

From the Gospel of Matthew, chapter 7

THE MOTE AND THE BEAM
Domenico Fetti (1589–1623)
The Metropolitan
Museum, New York

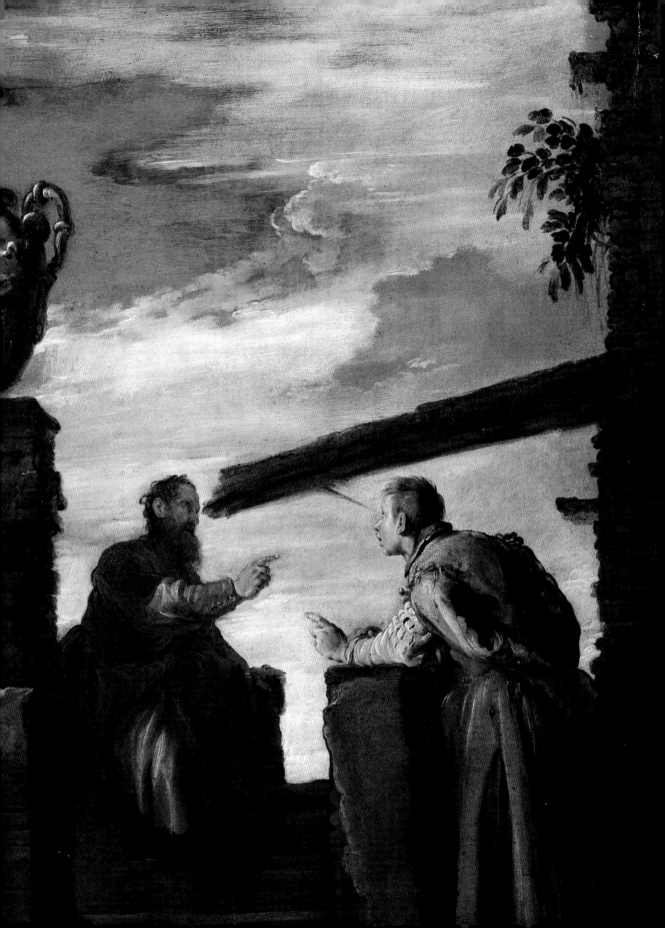

Domenico Fetti trained in Rome and worked in
Mantua before settling in Venice where he both
influenced and was influenced by other painters
of the Baroque period. He painted a series on the
parables of Jesus, most of which are in Dresden,
though this one is in New York. This scene is
one that it would have been very easy to treat in
a jejune manner, but Fetti has managed to give
it real power. This is partly the effect of the wild
sky and ruins, which bring out the tumult of
the argument in which one man is accusing the
other, who in turn tells him to look at his own
behaviour. The point is cleverly made by a beam
from the ruin jutting out and coming close to the
critic's eye.

In 1956, Her Majesty Queen Elizabeth reflected:

'Deep and acute differences, involving both intellect and emotion, are bound to arise between members of a family and also between friend and friend, and there is neither virtue nor value in pretending that they do not. In all such differences, however, there comes a moment when, for the sake of ultimate harmony, the healing power of tolerance, comradeship and love must be allowed to play its part.

'I speak of a tolerance that is not indifference, but is rather a willingness to recognize the possibility of right in others; of a comradeship that is not just a sentimental memory of good days past, but the certainty that the tried and staunch friends of yesterday are still in truth the same people today; of a love that can rise above anger and is ready to forgive.'

The sower

That same day Jesus went out of the house and sat beside the lake. Such great crowds gathered around him that he got into a boat and sat there, while the whole crowd stood on the beach. And he told them many things in parables, saying: 'Listen! A sower went out to sow. And as he sowed, some seeds fell on the path, and the birds came and ate them up. Other seeds fell on rocky ground, where they did not have much soil, and they sprang up quickly, since they had no depth of soil. But when the sun rose, they were scorched; and since they had no root, they withered away. Other seeds fell among thorns, and the thorns grew up and choked them. Other seeds fell on good soil and brought forth grain, some a hundredfold, some sixty, some thirty. Let anyone with ears listen!'

From the Gospel of Matthew, chapter 13

THE SOWER AT SUNSET
Vincent van Gogh (1853–90)
Kröller-Müller Museum,
Netherlands

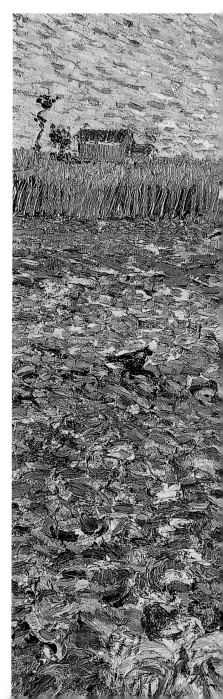

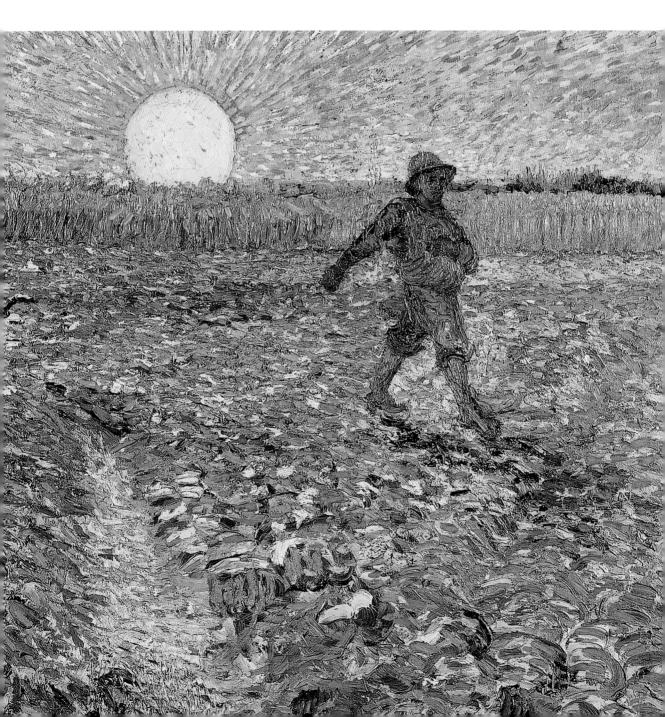

As a young man, Vincent van Gogh was intensely religious. Indeed he came to England to work as a missionary among miners. This intensity never left him and is one of the reasons his paintings have such an extraordinary drawing power. Sometimes this went with a slight sense of disturbance and potential darkness. And indeed something of that is in another version of the sower that van Gogh painted, in which a dark tree dominates the scene and the sower himself is in shadow. Just the opposite is the case in this version, which he painted in Arles in 1888. It is an effulgence of glory and joy. Even the earth on which the sower is scattering his seed is vibrant with potential life. While behind him, below the blazing sun, the wheat stands strong and bright.

The parable of Jesus, although it realistically observes that much of the seed fails, that which takes root in good soil brings forth grain, 'some a hundredfold, some sixty, some thirty' – in other words, such abundance outweighs the loss. It brings to mind another analogy of Jesus in which he compares the kingdom of God to a mustard seed, smaller than any other, which grows into a great tree (Mark chapter 4). Vincent van Gogh wonderfully conveys this sense of goodness flourishing.

In 1976, Her Majesty Queen Elizabeth reflected:

'Remember that good spreads outwards and every little does help. Mighty things from small beginnings grow. If there is reconciliation – if we can get the climate right – the good effects will flow much more quickly than most people would believe possible.

'Those who know the desert know also how quickly it can flower when the rains come. When the conflict stops, peace can blossom just as quickly.'

At home with the friends of Jesus

Now as they went on their way, he entered a
certain village, where a woman named Martha
welcomed him into her home. She had a sister
named Mary, who sat at the Lord's feet and
listened to what he was saying. But Martha was
distracted by her many tasks; so she came to him
and asked, 'Lord, do you not care that my sister
has left me to do all the work by myself? Tell her
then to help me.' But the Lord answered her,
'Martha, Martha, you are worried and distracted
by many things; there is need of only one thing.
Mary has chosen the better part, which will not
be taken away from her.'
From the Gospel of Luke, chapter 10

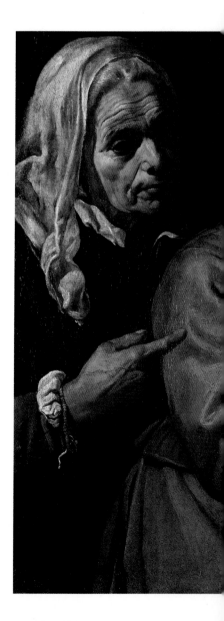

CHRIST IN THE HOUSE OF
MARTHA AND MARY
Diego Velázquez (1599–1660)
National Gallery, London

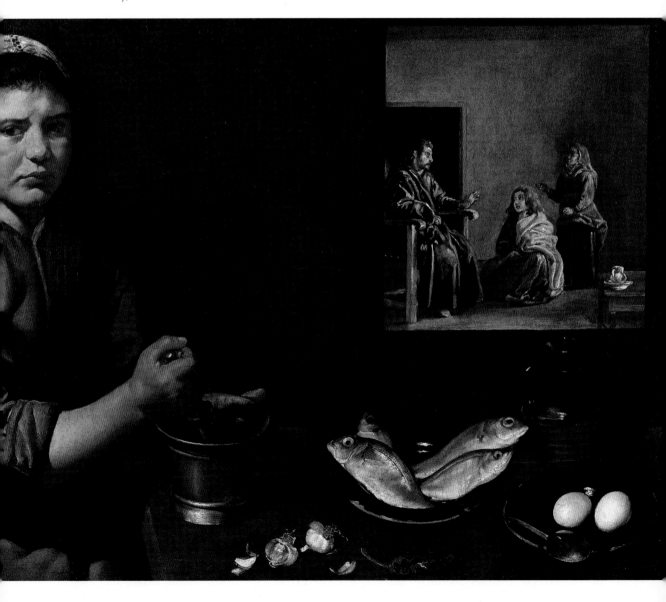

The scene is a kitchen, painted very realistically and probably based on the one in the artist's own home. The woman is perhaps making some garlic mayonnaise ready for the fish. But she is looking very disgruntled and facing directly forward as though to make her feelings known to the viewer. Behind her is an older woman not just whispering some advice but pointing. She is drawing attention to the Gospel scene set in the house of Martha and Mary. There is a discussion as to whether this is a painting or a mirror in which the painting is reflected, or a serving hatch into another room. The latest opinion is that the latter is most likely. My own view is that the older woman is reminding the maid of the scene which is as it were being pictured in her own mind.

The Gospel passage on which it is based has been a huge influence in the West as indicating the superiority of the contemplative way of life to the active. Martha, who is bustling about the house, is told, in words from the Authorised Version, 'But one thing is needful: and Mary hath chosen that good part, which shall not be taken away from her.' It is this passage that lay behind the growth of the monastic orders in the Middle Ages, especially the contemplative ones. At the same time there is an alternative tradition, which extols the practical sense of Martha as expressed for example in some of the mystery plays and then later by Martin Luther in his stress on the validity of the lay vocation. Perhaps the older woman is telling the younger one what George Herbert expressed in his poem 'The Elixir':

A servant with this clause
   Makes drudgery divine:
Who sweeps a room as for Thy laws,
   Makes that and th' action fine.

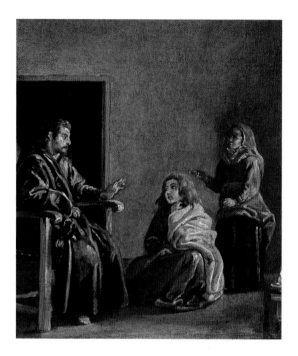

Martha, who is bustling about the house, is told,
in words from the Authorised Version, 'But one
thing is needful: and Mary hath chosen that good
part, which shall not be taken away from her.'

Jesus raises Lazarus

When Jesus arrived, he found that Lazarus had already been in the tomb for four days. Now Bethany was near Jerusalem, some two miles away, and many of the Jews had come to Martha and Mary to console them about their brother. When Martha heard that Jesus was coming, she went and met him, while Mary stayed at home. Martha said to Jesus, 'Lord, if you had been here, my brother would not have died. But even now I know that God will give you whatever you ask of him.' Jesus said to her, 'Your brother will rise again.' Martha said to him, 'I know that he will rise again in the resurrection on the last day.' Jesus said to her, 'I am the resurrection and the life. Those who believe in me, even though they die, will live, and everyone who lives and believes in me will never die. Do you believe this?' She said to him, 'Yes, Lord, I believe that you are the Messiah, the Son of God, the one coming into the world.'

When she had said this, she went back and called her sister Mary, and told her privately, 'The Teacher is here and is calling for you.' And when she heard it, she got up quickly and went to him. Now Jesus had not yet come to the village, but was still at the place where Martha had met him. The Jews who were with her in the house, consoling her, saw Mary get up quickly and go out. They followed her because they thought that she was going to the tomb to weep there.

When Mary came where Jesus was and saw him, she knelt at his feet and said to him, 'Lord, if you had been here, my brother would not have died.' When Jesus saw her weeping, and the Jews who came with her also weeping, he was greatly disturbed in spirit and deeply moved. He said, 'Where have you laid him?' They said to him, 'Lord, come and see.' Jesus began to weep. So the Jews said, 'See how he loved him!' But some of them said, 'Could not he who opened the eyes of the blind man have kept this man from dying?'

Then Jesus, again greatly disturbed, came to the tomb. It was a cave, and a stone was lying against it. Jesus said, 'Take away the stone.' Martha, the sister of the dead man, said to him, 'Lord, already there is a stench because he has been dead for four days.' Jesus said to her, 'Did I not tell you that if you believed, you would see the glory of God?' So they took away the stone. And Jesus looked upwards and said, 'Father, I thank you for having heard me. I knew that you always hear me, but I have said this for the sake of the crowd standing here, so that they may believe that you sent me.' When he had said this, he cried with a loud voice, 'Lazarus, come out!' The dead man came out, his hands and feet bound with strips of cloth, and his face wrapped in a cloth. Jesus said to them, 'Unbind him, and let him go.'

From the Gospel of John, chapter 11

THE RAISING OF LAZARUS
Duccio (c. 1255–60 – c. 1318–19)
Kimbell Art Museum, Fort Worth, USA

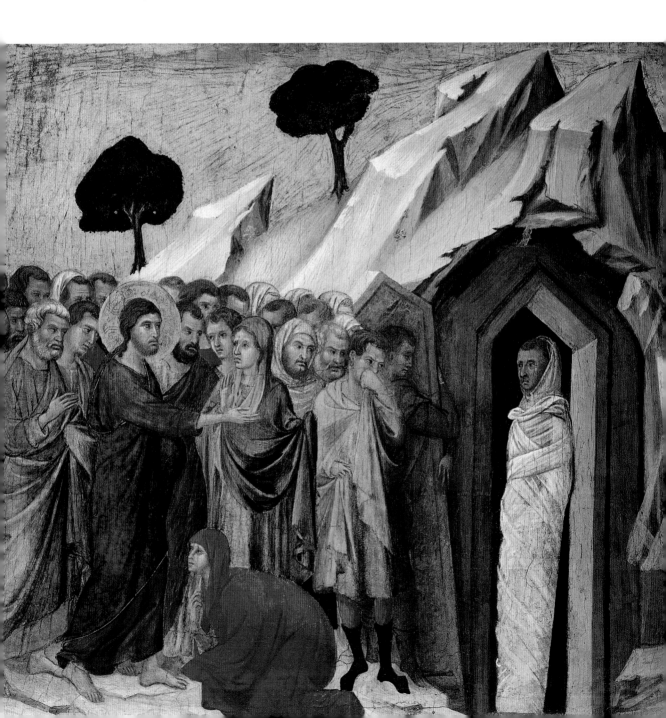

Duccio lived and died in Siena, and worked mostly there and in the surrounding Tuscany area. His main work is a large, double-sided altarpiece for the cathedral in the city, the *Maestà*, which he worked on from 1308 to 1311. On the front of this is an enthroned Madonna with child and various smaller scenes. On the back are 46 panels on the life of Christ and his mother. The difference between the front and the back is that, whereas the *Maestà* was for public viewing, the small panels like this one were for private devotion.

Duccio keeps closely to the Gospel story in its realism. The onlooker nearest the tomb, for example, is shown holding his nose because of the smell. The man behind him is shown removing the stone in front of the tomb. Lazarus stands bewildered, wrapped tight in his grave clothes. The eye moves from Lazarus across the scene to focus on Jesus with outstretched hand and arm saying to Lazarus, 'Come out', or 'Come forth' in the language of the Authorised Version. Mary Magdalene, identified in red, kneels at the feet of Jesus. In the early Christian tradition the three different Marys in the Gospels are identified as the Magdalene, but the Mary who lived with her sister Martha may in fact have been a different one. Martha stands, holding her cloak, looking wonderingly at Jesus. Behind Jesus with white hair is Peter. All around, the crowd presses to see what is going on, each face different and delicately painted.

The theme of the painting is well conveyed in the contrast between the stark white of the barren rocks and Lazarus's grave clothes, and the green growth of the trees arising from the rocks. Life from death.

This is one of the earliest scenes in the Gospels to be painted and it appears on the walls of the catacombs in Rome in the third and fourth centuries. The catacombs were the places where the early Christians were buried. The raising of Lazarus expressed the hope that they too would rise from the dead, in their case not to a continuing life on earth but to everlasting life in a new form and dimension. Duccio shared that hope and sublimely expresses it.

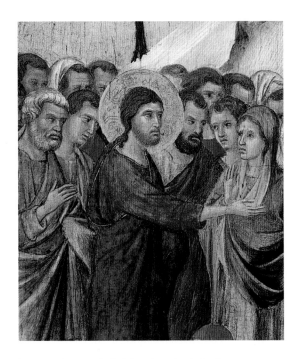

Martha stands, holding her cloak, looking
wonderingly at Jesus. Behind Jesus with
white hair is Peter. All around, the crowd
presses to see what is going on, each
face different and delicately painted.

Jesus protects a vulnerable woman

Then each of them went home while Jesus went to the Mount of Olives. Early in the morning he came again to the temple. All the people came to him and he sat down and began to teach them. The scribes and the Pharisees brought a woman who had been caught in adultery; and making her stand before all of them, they said to him, 'Teacher, this woman was caught in the very act of committing adultery. Now in the law Moses commanded us to stone such women. Now what do you say?' They said this to test him, so that they might have some charge to bring against him. Jesus bent down and wrote with his finger on the ground. When they kept on questioning him, he straightened up and said to them, 'Let anyone among you who is without sin be the first to throw a stone at her.' And once again he bent down and wrote on the ground. When they heard it, they went away, one by one, beginning with the elders; and Jesus was left alone with the woman standing before him. Jesus straightened up and said to her, 'Woman, where are they? Has no one condemned you?' She said, 'No one, sir.' And Jesus said, 'Neither do I condemn you. Go your way, and from now on do not sin again.'

From the Gospel of John, chapter 8

CHRIST AND THE WOMAN TAKEN IN ADULTERY
Max Beckmann (1884–1950)
St Louis Art Museum

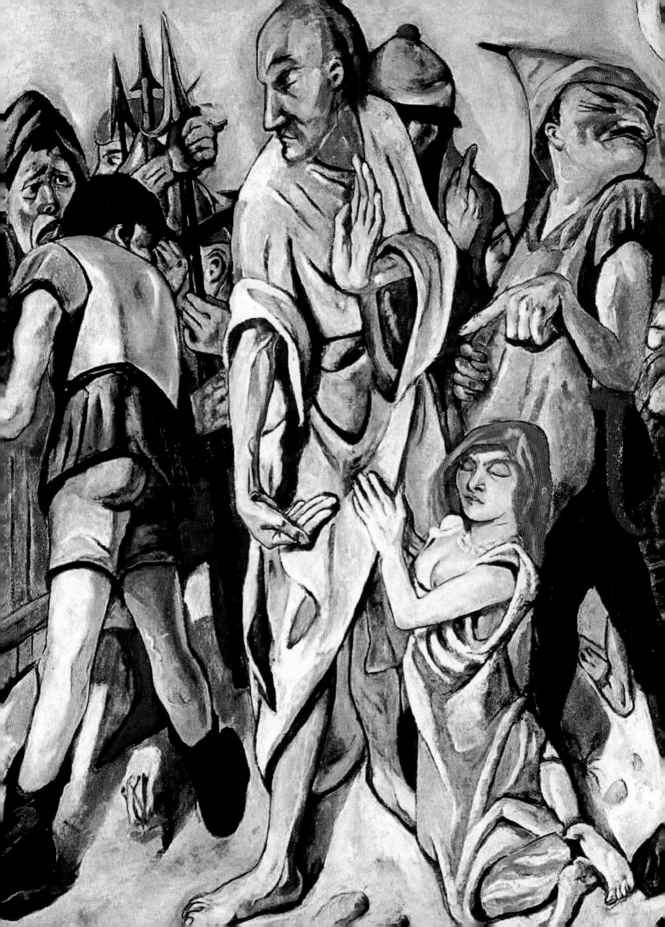

Max Beckmann was often described as an
expressionist, but he rejected this term, as
he also rejected abstract painting. He was a
member of a group known as 'New objectivity'
but his objectivity stands in the tradition of
painters like Matthias Grünwald, Bruegel and
Bosch with their sometimes brutal depictions of
their subjects. He was very well thought of in
Germany before the rise of Hitler, who rejected
his work and that of most other modern painters
as degenerate.

This painting of 1917 clearly reflects
Beckmann's turn away from classical ideas
of beauty, as well as his experience of the
First World War, as a result of which he had
a breakdown. It shows Christ protecting the
kneeling woman from an ugly mob, some with
spears, and one on the left with stones in his
hand. It is very much a painting of the hands:
the pointing hands of the self-righteous accuser
on the right, the praying hands of the woman
and the hands of Christ taking an unusual form.
His left hand, palm open, as it were holds the
crowd at bay, while the right one, cupped just
by the praying hands of the woman, suggests a
refuge in which she will be enveloped and safe.

In 2011, Her Majesty Queen Elizabeth reflected:

'Although we are capable of great acts of kindness, history teaches us that we sometimes need saving from ourselves. God sent into the world a unique person – neither a philosopher nor a general (important though they are) – but a Saviour, with the power to forgive.

'Forgiveness lies at the heart of the Christian faith. It can heal broken families, it can restore friendships and it can reconcile divided communities. It is in forgiveness that we feel the power of God's love.'

Jesus welcomes children

People were bringing little children to him in order that he might touch them; and the disciples spoke sternly to them. But when Jesus saw this, he was indignant and said to them, 'Let the little children come to me; do not stop them; for it is to such as these that the kingdom of God belongs. Truly I tell you, whoever does not receive the kingdom of God as a little child will never enter it.' And he took them up in his arms, laid his hands on them, and blessed them.

From the Gospel of Mark, chapter 10

**CHRIST BLESSES
THE CHILDREN**
Artemisia Gentileschi
(1593–1653)
San Carlo al Corso, Rome

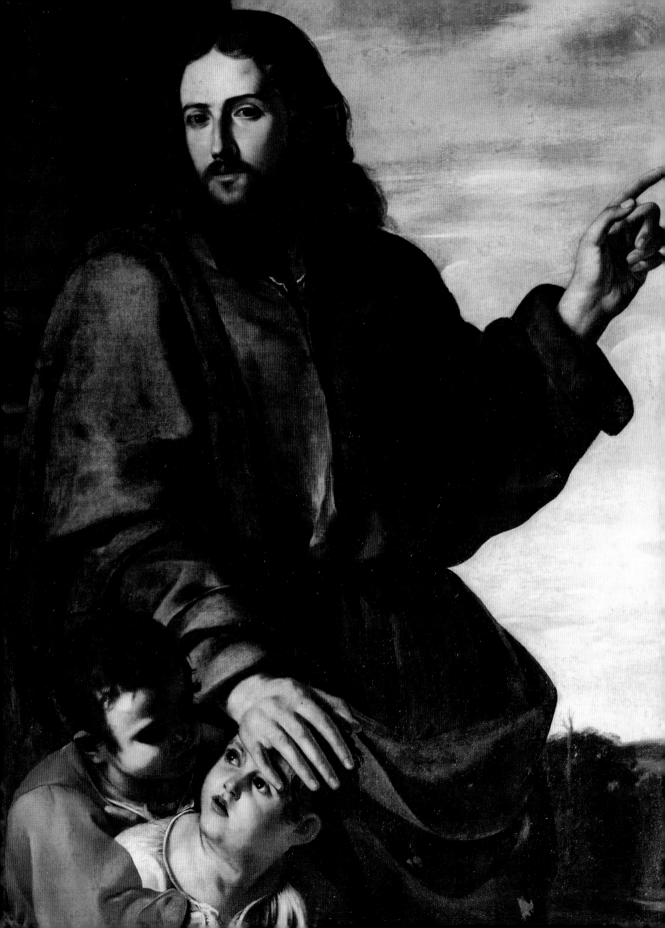

Having been totally overshadowed by male
painters for centuries, Artemisia Gentileschi is
now recognized as one of the major artists of
the Baroque period. She is best known for her
paintings of strong women, often in scenes of
violence, and this is one of her rare paintings
on a Gospel scene. Influenced by Caravaggio,
she uses strong contrasts and bold outlines to
create a sense of drama. Here the major contrast
is between the dark background and figure of
Christ on the left and the bright sky on the
right. Depictions of this scene by other artists
focus on the blessing of the children. In this
painting, that is balanced by the pointing finger
against the sky. This is to bring out the second
theme in the Gospel account. The first is that
Christ, in contrast to other adults round him,
welcomed and blessed children. The second is
that we have to receive the kingdom of God like
a child, that is, with simple acceptance. So Jesus
points, indicating that he is teaching and that this
teaching is directed towards helping people enter
the kingdom.

This is reinforced by the way Christ looks
directly at the viewer with a sense of authority,
making it clear that, 'Yes, it is you the viewer who
has to become like a child.' The light is on the
children, one of whom is looking heavenward, to
the true light of which the light in the painting is
a sign.

In 1984, Her Majesty the Queen reflected:

'It is particularly at Christmas, which marks the birth of the Prince of Peace, that we should work to heal old wounds and to abandon prejudice and suspicion. What better way of making a start than by remembering what Christ said: "Except ye become as little children, ye shall not enter into the Kingdom of Heaven."'

The two sons

Then Jesus said, 'There was a man who had two sons. The younger of them said to his father, "Father, give me the share of the property that will belong to me." So he divided his property between them. A few days later the younger son gathered all he had and travelled to a distant country, and there he squandered his property in dissolute living. When he had spent everything, a severe famine took place throughout that country, and he began to be in need.

So he went and hired himself out to one of the citizens of that country, who sent him to his fields to feed the pigs. He would gladly have filled himself with the pods that the pigs were eating; and no one gave him anything. But when he came to himself he said, "How many of my father's hired hands have bread enough and to spare, but here I am dying of hunger! I will get up and go to my father, and I will say to him, 'Father, I have sinned against heaven and before you; I am no longer worthy to be called your son; treat me like one of your hired hands.'" So he set off and went to his father. But while he was still far off, his father saw him and was filled with compassion; he ran and put his arms around him and kissed him. Then the son said to him, "Father, I have sinned against heaven and before you; I am no longer worthy to be called your son." But the father said to his slaves, "Quickly, bring out a robe—the best one—and put it on

him; put a ring on his finger and sandals on his feet. And get the fatted calf and kill it, and let us eat and celebrate; for this son of mine was dead and is alive again; he was lost and is found!" And they began to celebrate.

'Now his elder son was in the field; and when he came and approached the house, he heard music and dancing. He called one of the slaves and asked what was going on. He replied, "Your brother has come, and your father has killed the fatted calf, because he has got him back safe and sound." Then he became angry and refused to go in. His father came out and began to plead with him. But he answered his father, "Listen! For all these years I have been working like a slave for you, and I have never disobeyed your command; yet you have never given me even a young goat so that I might celebrate with my friends. But when this son of yours came back, who has devoured your property with prostitutes, you killed the fatted calf for him!" Then the father said to him, "Son, you are always with me, and all that is mine is yours. But we had to celebrate and rejoice, because this brother of yours was dead and has come to life; he was lost and has been found."'

From the Gospel of Luke, chapter 15

> **THE RETURN OF THE**
> **PRODIGAL SON**
> Rembrandt (1606–69)
> The Hermitage, St Petersburg

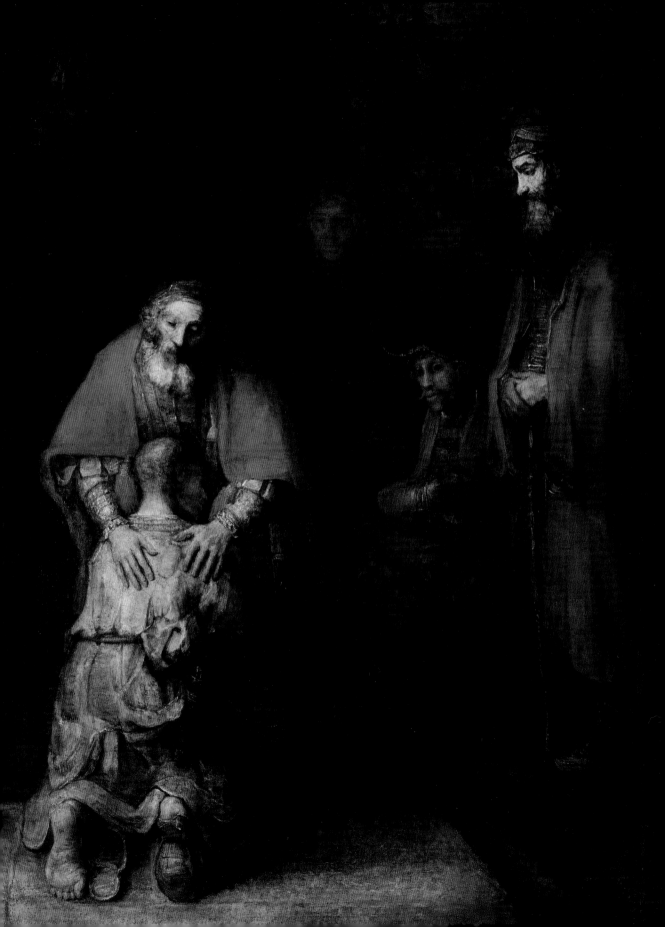

The focus in this painting is first of all on the father embracing his son. This is the person who asked for his inheritance early, disappeared to Egypt and quickly got through the money. To keep himself alive he got a job looking after pigs, and even so he was starving. Then 'he came to himself' and realized he would be far better off even as one of his father's servants. So he resolved to say sorry and go home.

The father had never given up on his son. Every day he scanned the horizon to see if his son would come home. Then, suddenly, there he was. An intimate embrace conveyed all that needed to be said. The son, his clothes all ragged, his shoes worn and his feet calloused, is hugged close in a silence that says it all.

In his book *The Return of the Prodigal Son*, Henri Nouwen reflects on this painting and notes that one of the hands is that of a woman. He suggests that this reflects the feminine side of divine love, so God can be said to love like a mother as well as a father.

This story is usually called 'The prodigal son'. But there are two sons in the script, not just one. Standing at one side is the elder brother, as stiff as the rod in his hand. Background figures look on, similarly disapproving at the fuss being made of the profligate young son, unwilling to share in the rejoicing. So the elder brother complains that a similar party had never been given for him, even though he had stayed at home and done his duty over many years. To him the Father says, 'Son, you are always with me, and all that is mine is yours.' Both sons are loved.

The early paintings of Rembrandt are grandiose but later, after much suffering, he painted in a much quieter, more tender style. There may be particular paternal feeling in this painting as all his children except one, Titus, died young, and even Titus died before Rembrandt himself.

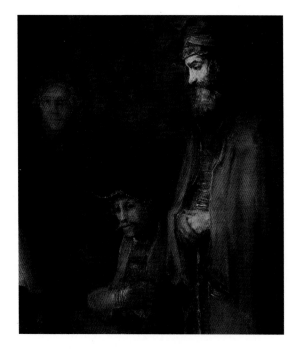

This story is usually called 'The prodigal son'.
But there are two sons in the script, not just
one. Standing at one side is the elder brother,
as stiff as the rod in his hand. Background
figures look on, similarly disapproving at
the fuss being made of the profligate young
son, unwilling to share in the rejoicing.

Jesus is transfigured

THE TRANSFIGURATION
Sixth-century mosaic
St Catherine's monastery, Sinai

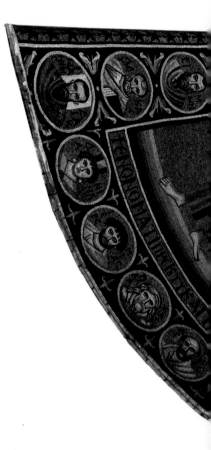

Six days later, Jesus took with him Peter and
James and John, and led them up a high
mountain apart, by themselves. And he was
transfigured before them, and his clothes became
dazzling white, such as no one on earth could
bleach them. And there appeared to them Elijah
with Moses, who were talking with Jesus. Then
Peter said to Jesus, 'Rabbi, it is good for us to be
here; let us make three dwellings, one for you,
one for Moses, and one for Elijah.' He did not
know what to say, for they were terrified. Then
a cloud overshadowed them, and from the cloud
there came a voice, 'This is my Son, the Beloved;
listen to him!' Suddenly when they looked
around, they saw no one with them any more,
but only Jesus.

From the Gospel of Mark, chapter 9

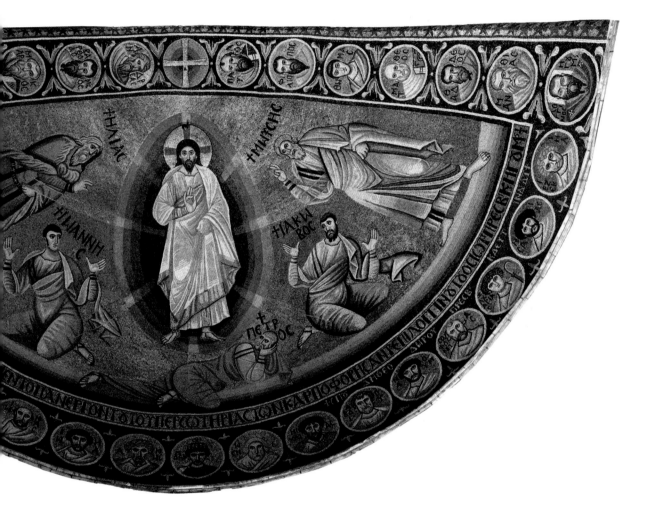

From 726 to 842 almost every religious image in the Christian world was destroyed, in the period known as iconoclasm. Miraculously a tiny number survived, mainly at St Catherine's monastery in Sinai, which because of its remoteness was cut off from the power struggles of the day. This superb mosaic is one that survived. It shows Christ in a blue mandorla transfigured into a figure of glory, and blessing the world with his open hand. Below him, turning away awestruck, are the three Apostles who went up the mountain with him, Peter at the bottom, James on the right as we look, and John on the left.

Standing to the left of Christ is Elijah the prophet and, to the right, Moses the giver of the law. The meaning of the scene for the New Testament writers is that both the prophetic tradition in Judaism and its law find their fulfilment in the one declared by God to be 'the beloved son'. The scene is also referred to in St Peter's second letter, chapter 1:

For we did not follow cleverly devised myths when we made known to you the power and coming of our Lord Jesus Christ, but we had been eyewitnesses of his majesty. For he received honour and glory from God the Father when that voice was conveyed to him by the Majestic Glory, saying, 'This is my Son, my Beloved, with whom I am well pleased.' We ourselves heard this voice come from heaven, while we were with him on the holy mountain.

For St Paul, the vocation of all Christians, and potentially all human beings, is to be transfigured. As he wrote:

And all of us, with unveiled faces, seeing the glory of the Lord as though reflected in a mirror, are being transformed into the same image from one degree of glory to another; for this comes from the Lord, the Spirit.
From St Paul's second letter to the Corinthians, chapter 3

In 2013, Her Majesty Queen Elizabeth reflected:

'For Christians, as for all people of faith, reflection, meditation and prayer help us to renew ourselves in God's love, as we strive daily to become better people. The Christmas message shows us that this love is for everyone. There is no one beyond its reach.'

4
MAN OF
SORROWS

'Christ not only revealed to us the truth in his teachings. He lived by what he believed and gave us the strength to try to do the same – and, finally, on the cross, he showed the supreme example of physical and moral courage.'

The Queen's Christmas broadcast, 1981

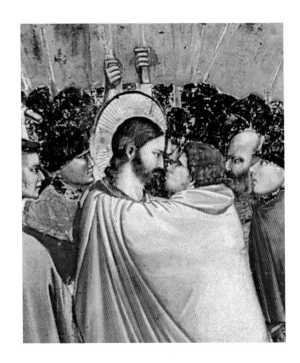

Jesus enters Jerusalem

When they had come near Jerusalem and had reached Bethphage, at the Mount of Olives, Jesus sent two disciples, saying to them, 'Go into the village ahead of you, and immediately you will find a donkey tied, and a colt with her; untie them and bring them to me. If anyone says anything to you, just say this, "The Lord needs them." And he will send them immediately.' This took place to fulfil what had been spoken through the prophet, saying,

> 'Tell the daughter of Zion,
> Look, your king is coming to you,
> humble, and mounted on a donkey,
> and on a colt, the foal of a donkey.'

The disciples went and did as Jesus had directed them; they brought the donkey and the colt, and put their cloaks on them, and he sat on them. A very large crowd spread their cloaks on the road, and others cut branches from the trees and spread them on the road. The crowds that went ahead of him and that followed were shouting,

> 'Hosanna to the Son of David!
> Blessed is the one who comes in the name of the Lord!
> Hosanna in the highest heaven!'

When he entered Jerusalem, the whole city was in turmoil, asking, 'Who is this?' The crowds were saying, 'This is the prophet Jesus from Nazareth in Galilee.'

From the Gospel of Matthew, chapter 21

THE ENTRY INTO JERUSALEM
Twelfth-century fresco
Panagia Asinou Church, Cyprus

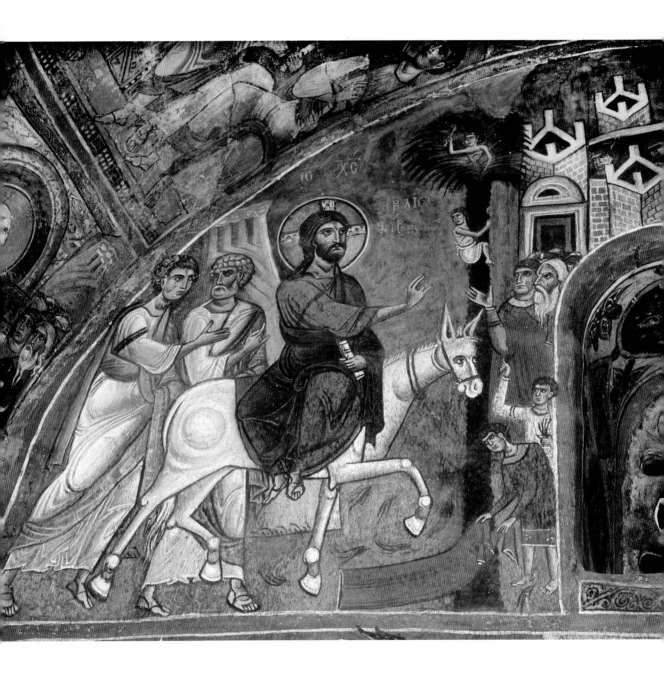

In Cyprus there are a number of churches that
look nothing from the outside but within each of
them can be seen a heaven of beautiful frescoes.
For many centuries the island was under Arab
domination and churches were deliberately
inconspicuous, some with low sloping roofs. But it
was a time when Byzantine art was at its height,
and workmen from workshops in Constantinople
painted here and in other churches round the
empire. The frescoes at Asinou are particularly
glorious, and the church is a world heritage site.

This is a traditional rendering of Christ's entry
into Jerusalem, based on the Gospel account.
Jesus rides side-saddle on a white donkey as a
King of Peace. His outstretched arm and hand
bless the city of Jerusalem whose fine buildings
are to the right. One man throws a cloak on
the road, another holds a branch in his hand,
while others climb up the palm tree to cut down
fresh branches to strew on the way. The tree
also provides a fine vantage point to see the
procession below. Two of the Apostles, the one
with white hair being Peter, walk beside the
donkey. From the town a few faces glare out,
clearly not prepared to welcome Christ.

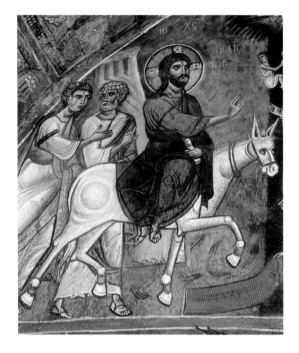

Jesus rides side-saddle on a white donkey
as a King of Peace. His outstretched arm
and hand bless the city of Jerusalem.

Jesus reclaims the Temple for God

Then Jesus entered the temple and drove out all
who were selling and buying in the temple, and
he overturned the tables of the money-changers
and the seats of those who sold doves. He said to
them, 'It is written,

"My house shall be called a house of prayer";
but you are making it a den of robbers.'

From the Gospel of Matthew, chapter 21

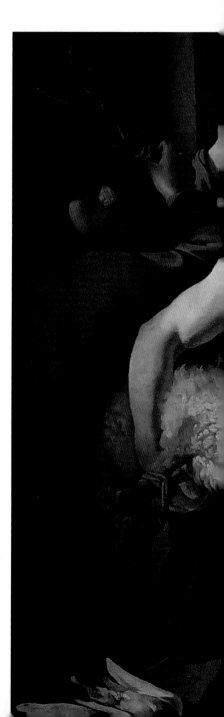

CHRIST DRIVING THE MONEY-CHANGERS FROM THE TEMPLE
Dirck van Baburen (1595–1624)
Private collection

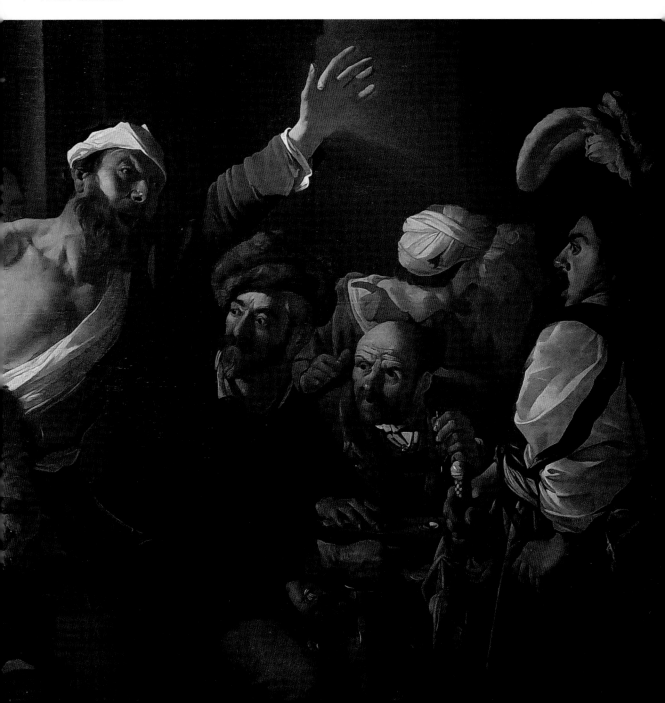

Dirck van Baburen was a Dutch painter who belonged to a group of fellow artists all happy to be influenced by Caravaggio, known as the Utrecht Caravaggisti. He died at the age of 33. This fine work was only rediscovered as his work in 1996.

The scene of Christ driving out the traders only became frequent in art after the Council of Trent (1545–63), which sought to drive corruption out of the Church. Its most famous depictions are by El Greco, which show Christ, whip in hand, urging the traders out with a violent energy. This one by van Baburen is no less dramatic but is interestingly different. Christ does not have a whip. Instead he simply holds out his arm, palm open as though to say 'Stop'. The faces and hands of the money-changers are very expressive, all indicating how grasping they are over money. They wear rich fur hats or feathers. By contrast, Christ is almost naked, with a shawl over one shoulder and a simple white headdress. On the bottom left the doves that were offered are laid out. Most prominent of all is the fact that Jesus is carrying a lamb, a detail not mentioned in the text, but clearly indicating for the artist and viewer at the time that Jesus himself is the lamb of God who will be offered in sacrifice for the sins of the whole world.

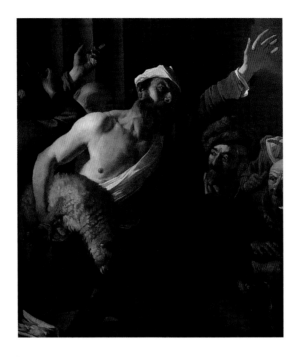

Jesus is carrying a lamb, a detail not mentioned
in the text, but clearly indicating for the artist
and viewer at the time that Jesus himself is
the lamb of God who will be offered in
sacrifice for the sins of the whole world.

A last meal together

When it was evening, he took his place with the twelve; and while they were eating, he said, 'Truly I tell you, one of you will betray me.' And they became greatly distressed and began to say to him one after another, 'Surely not I, Lord?' He answered, 'The one who has dipped his hand into the bowl with me will betray me. The Son of Man goes as it is written of him, but woe to that one by whom the Son of Man is betrayed! It would have been better for that one not to have been born.' Judas, who betrayed him, said, 'Surely not I, Rabbi?' He replied, 'You have said so.'

While they were eating, Jesus took a loaf of bread, and after blessing it he broke it, gave it to the disciples, and said, 'Take, eat; this is my body.' Then he took a cup, and after giving thanks he gave it to them, saying, 'Drink from it, all of you; for this is my blood of the covenant, which is poured out for many for the forgiveness of sins. I tell you, I will never again drink of this fruit of the vine until that day when I drink it new with you in my Father's kingdom.'
From the Gospel of Matthew, chapter 26

THE LAST SUPPER
Ugolino da Siena (1280?– 1349)
Metropolitan Museum, New York

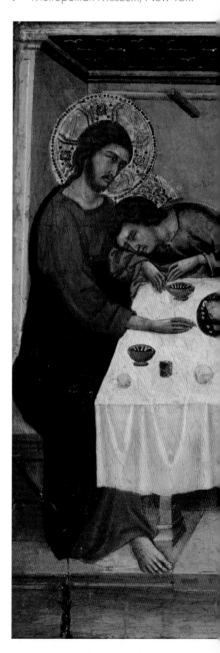

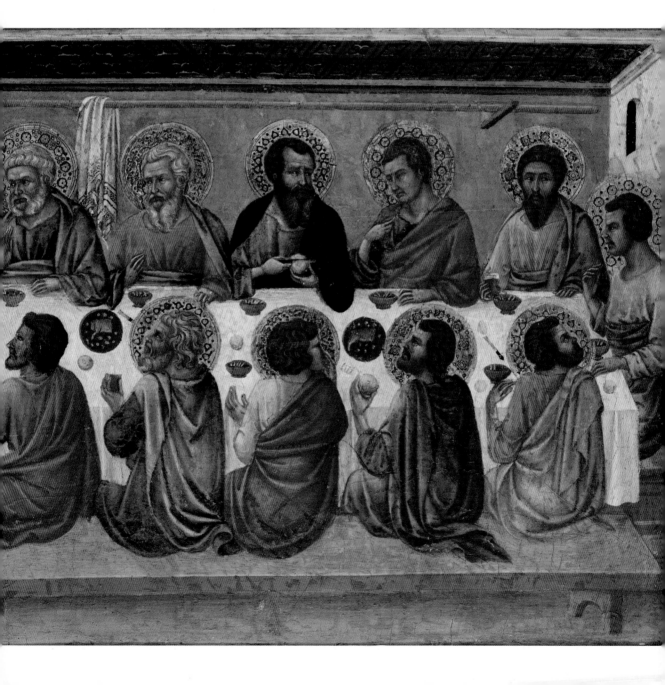

Ugolino di Nerio, the artist's proper name, was born into a family of painters and was responsible for spreading Sienese influence in Florence, where he was commissioned to paint in Santa Croce and Santa Maria Novella. He was heavily influenced by Duccio, and some of his work is clearly derived from Duccio's *Maestà*, but he came to develop much more of a style of his own using brighter colours, as in this painting. This depiction of the Last Supper was the left-hand painting of seven panels in the predella (the lowest part of the altarpiece) of Santa Croce.

The 12 Apostles sit either side of a long table, of the kind that would be found in the refectory of any monastery. Their haloes are prominent and heavily embossed. To the left on the near side, without a halo, is Judas. Jesus has told them that one of them will betray him. Judas turns to Jesus with his arm gesticulating to say, 'Surely not I, Rabbi?' Leaning on the shoulder of Jesus is the beloved disciple, with Peter next to him. The disciples, all with different, questioning faces, are reflecting on what this might mean and who it would be.

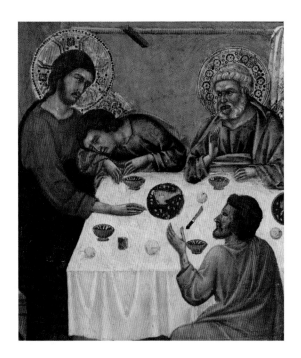

The 12 Apostles sit either side of a long table, of
the kind that would be found in the refectory
of any monastery. Their haloes are prominent
and heavily embossed. To the left on the near
side, without a halo, is Judas. Jesus has told them
that one of them will betray him. Judas turns to
Jesus with his arm gesticulating to say, 'Surely
not I, Rabbi?' Leaning on the shoulder of Jesus
is the beloved disciple, with Peter next to him.

Facing suffering and death

He came out and went, as was his custom, to
the Mount of Olives; and the disciples followed
him. When he reached the place, he said to
them, 'Pray that you may not come into the time
of trial.' Then he withdrew from them about a
stone's throw, knelt down, and prayed, 'Father, if
you are willing, remove this cup from me; yet, not
my will but yours be done.' Then an angel from
heaven appeared to him and gave him strength.
In his anguish he prayed more earnestly, and his
sweat became like great drops of blood falling
down on the ground. When he got up from
prayer, he came to the disciples and found them
sleeping because of grief, and he said to them,
'Why are you sleeping? Get up and pray that you
may not come into the time of trial.'
From the Gospel of Luke, chapter 22

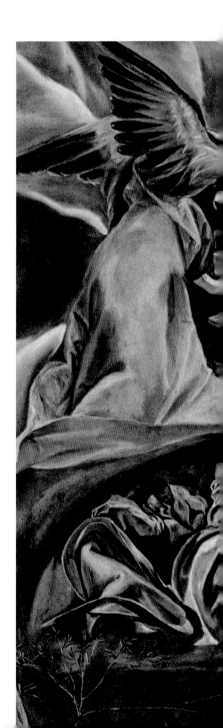

THE AGONY IN THE GARDEN
El Greco (1541 – 1614)
Toledo Museum of
Art, Toledo, Ohio

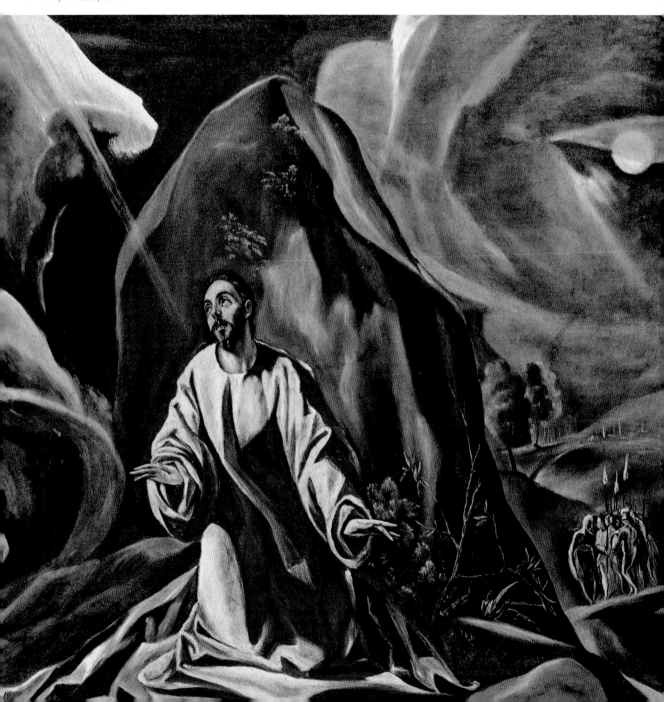

El Greco's real name was Domenicos Theotokopoulos but he has always been known as 'The Greek'. He originally trained and worked as an icon writer (for, strictly speaking, icons are written not painted) in Crete, which, after the fall of Constantinople in 1453, was the centre of Post-Byzantine art. At the age of 26, like other Byzantine artists, he moved to Venice and then to Rome where he opened a workshop. In Italy he was influenced by the artists of the High Renaissance, including Tintoretto. He then went on to Toledo where he received a number of notable commissions. Something of El Greco's original vocation as an icon writer can be seen in this and other of his paintings, both in their form and spiritual intensity. His dramatic expressionist style was much appreciated in the twentieth century, anticipating as it did some of the artistic trends of modernism.

In this painting there is no attempt to depict the scene in the Garden as it might have looked to the eye. Instead it is divided into four segments. To the right, lurking in the background, indicating what lies ahead, is a group round Judas. They gather beneath a billowing sky and pale moon which throws its haunting light on the landscape. To the left, almost enclosed in a shell, are the three Apostles trying, and failing, to keep awake. Then in the centre, dominating the scene, behind a great brown rock acting as a hood, is Jesus praying that he might not have to drink the cup of suffering. He is looking up at the angel, who holds out the cup. Jesus did not want to commit suicide. He

did not want to die. He prayed that he might not have to. But he recognized what would happen if he continued to take his message about the kingdom of God to the heart of the political and religious establishment. So whatever might come, 'not my will but yours be done'.

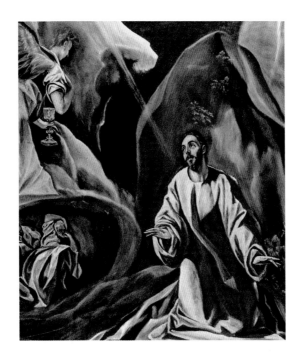

In the centre, dominating the scene, behind a great brown rock acting as a hood, is Jesus praying that he might not have to drink the cup of suffering. He is looking up at the angel, who holds out the cup.

Betrayed

While he was still speaking, Judas, one of the twelve, arrived; with him was a large crowd with swords and clubs, from the chief priests and the elders of the people. Now the betrayer had given them a sign, saying, 'The one I will kiss is the man; arrest him.' At once he came up to Jesus and said, 'Greetings, Rabbi!' and kissed him. Jesus said to him, 'Friend, do what you are here to do.' Then they came and laid hands on Jesus and arrested him. Suddenly, one of those with Jesus put his hand on his sword, drew it, and struck the slave of the high priest, cutting off his ear. Then Jesus said to him, 'Put your sword back into its place; for all who take the sword will perish by the sword. Do you think that I cannot appeal to my Father, and he will at once send me more than twelve legions of angels? But how then would the scriptures be fulfilled, which say it must happen in this way?' At that hour Jesus said to the crowds, 'Have you come out with swords and clubs to arrest me as though I were a bandit? Day after day I sat in the temple teaching, and you did not arrest me. But all this has taken place, so that the scriptures of the prophets may be fulfilled.' Then all the disciples deserted him and fled.

From the Gospel of Matthew, chapter 26

THE BETRAYAL OF CHRIST
Giotto (1267–1337)
The Scrovegni Chapel, Padua

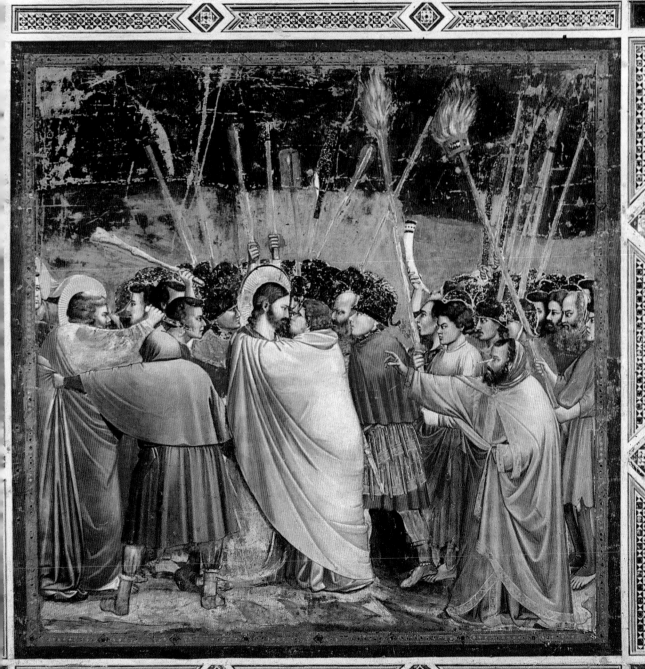

The whole of the Scrovegni Chapel in Padua is
covered in frescoes by Giotto. They depict scenes
from the life of Christ and the life of Mary, and
are regarded as one of the defining works of
Western art. For according to contemporaries
it was Giotto who first developed a naturalistic
style, his painting being much closer to life than
the more stylized work of earlier artists. At the
same time, there is a strong devotional element
in his work. In later, more technically advanced
painting, this became lost or at least transformed
into work that sought greater realism and
more obvious drama. As in Duccio, discussed
below, there is still a tender piety expressed in
his paintings.

In this fresco, however, the emphasis is on the
drama. The dark and light shades of blue above
the dark trees create a menacing effect. There is
violence in the air as spears, burning flares and
sticks are brandished against the sky. The faces
are fierce, as hands are pointed and clothes are
grabbed. An armed mob in all its fury. To the left
of the picture one of the disciples cuts off the ear
of the high priest's servant.

The central focus, however, is on Judas
enveloping Jesus in his cloak and kissing him.
Jesus looks Judas straight in the eyes and
addresses him as 'Friend'.

In 2015, Her Majesty the Queen reflected:

'Despite being displaced and persecuted throughout his short life, Christ's unchanging message was not one of revenge or violence but simply that we should love one another. Although it is not an easy message to follow, we shouldn't be discouraged; rather, it inspires us to try harder: to be thankful for the people who bring love and happiness into our own lives, and to look for ways of spreading that love to others, whenever and wherever we can.'

Jesus and political power

When morning came, all the chief priests and the elders of the people conferred together against Jesus in order to bring about his death. They bound him, led him away, and handed him over to Pilate the governor . . .

Now Jesus stood before the governor, and the governor asked him, 'Are you the king of the Jews?' Jesus said, 'You say so.' But when he was accused by the chief priests and elders, he did not answer. Then Pilate said to him, 'Do you not hear how many accusations they make against you?' But he gave him no answer, not even to a single charge, so that the governor was greatly amazed.

Now at the festival the governor was accustomed to release a prisoner for the crowd, anyone whom they wanted. At that time they had a notorious prisoner called Jesus Barabbas. So after they had gathered, Pilate said to them, 'Whom do you want me to release for you, Jesus Barabbas or Jesus who is called the Messiah?' For he realized that it was out of jealousy that they had handed him over. While he was sitting on the judgement seat, his wife sent word to him, 'Have nothing to do with that innocent man, for today I have suffered a great deal because of a dream about him.' Now the chief priests and the elders persuaded the crowds to ask for Barabbas and to have Jesus killed. The governor again said to them, 'Which of the two do you want me to release for you?' And they said, 'Barabbas. Pilate said to them, 'Then what should I do with Jesus who is called the Messiah? All of them said, 'Let him be crucified!' Then he asked, 'Why, what evil has he done?' But they shouted all the more, 'Let him be crucified!'

So when Pilate saw that he could do nothing but rather that a riot was beginning, he took some water and washed his hands before the crowd, saying, 'I am innocent of this man's blood; see to it yourselves.'

From the Gospel of Matthew, chapter 27

Man of sorrows
Jesus and political power
127

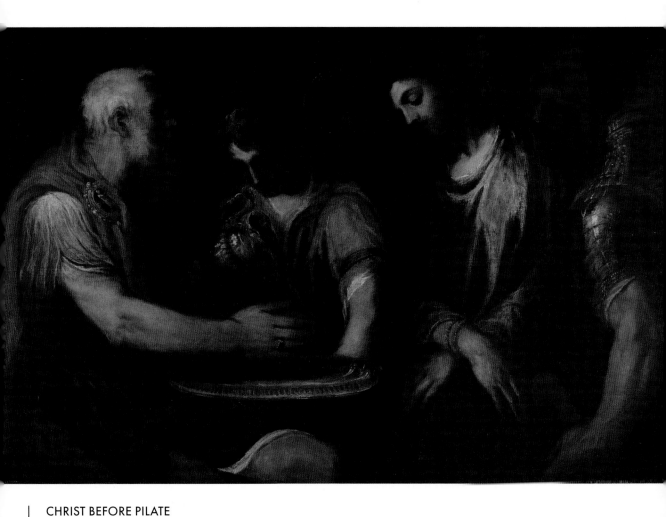

CHRIST BEFORE PILATE
Andrea Schiavone (1500–63)
Royal Collection

Andrea Meldolla, to give the artist his real name, was born and brought up in Croatia, and was as a result given the name Schiavone, meaning 'Slav'. Croatia was part of the large Venetian sea empire and was ruled by the Republic of Venice, and it was to Venice that Schiavone went to live and work. Art historians term him a mannerist, that is, one who concentrates on style rather than realism, but one deeply influenced by painters of the late Renaissance such as Giorgione and Titian. He was admired by the Stuarts and although out of fashion for many centuries he has come more into focus in recent years.

This painting has some figures in the background who are difficult to make out and the eye is drawn to the areas in it where light falls. To the right, it is on the muscular arm and heavy armour of the soldier, indicating the element of coercion so present in human life, especially public life. Pilate is protected and Jesus is in captivity because of the threat of that force. By contrast, Jesus stands submissive, with his head in prayerful repose and his hands, though bound, relaxed. The servant next to him, like all servants, is half hidden and simply doing what he is told, washing the hands of Pilate. Pilate himself, pictured as an aged man with balding white hair, looks across at Jesus as he holds out his hands to have water poured over them.

The power of this painting is the way it captures an intimate moment in a public drama. Outside, the crowds are milling and shouting. Elsewhere in the building, soldiers and officials are going about their business. But here is one

of those hidden moments in which destiny is made. Pilate, like so many in every age, not least our own, shuffles off responsibility to others. Not surprisingly the phrase 'I wash my hands of it' has become part of the language.

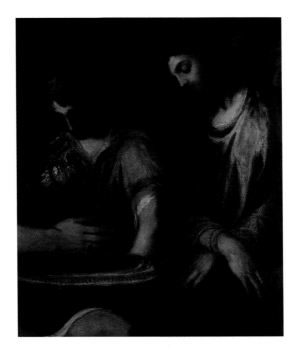

Jesus stands submissive, with his head in prayerful repose and his hands, though bound, relaxed. The servant next to him, like all servants, is half hidden and simply doing what he is told, washing the hands of Pilate.

Jesus is mocked

Then the soldiers of the governor took Jesus into the governor's headquarters, and they gathered the whole cohort around him. They stripped him and put a scarlet robe on him, and after twisting some thorns into a crown, they put it on his head. They put a reed in his right hand and knelt before him and mocked him, saying, 'Hail, King of the Jews!' They spat on him, and took the reed and struck him on the head. After mocking him, they stripped him of the robe and put his own clothes on him. Then they led him away to crucify him.

From the Gospel of Matthew, chapter 27

**JESUS IS MOCKED
BY SOLDIERS**
Georges Rouault (1871 – 1958)
Museum of Modern Art, New York

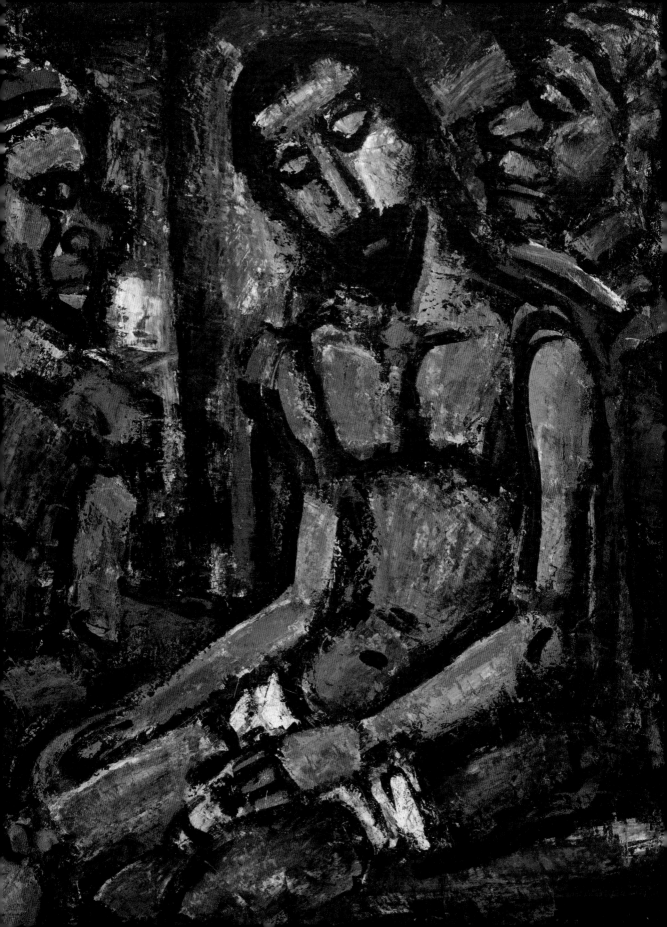

Georges Rouault was highly sensitive to the anguish of the world and was particularly affected by the terrible suffering caused by the First World War. He originally trained as a stained-glass artist, and this can be recognized in his work. The heavy black lines in the painting, acting like lead in glass windows, accentuate the sense of the dark side of life. A devout Roman Catholic he was also highly aware of the masks we wear, and in his portraits of clowns and judges showed what lies behind these masks.

In this scene of the mocking, Jesus sits quietly and submissively while behind him, either side of the column, two soldiers glare with menace.

In art, the depiction of Christ at the Column is a variation of the scene of the flagellation of Christ, or scourging at the pillar, both being closely linked with Christ's mocking. The scene first appears in the West in the ninth century in illuminated manuscripts and ivories and became prominent in the fifteenth century, perhaps because of the Franciscan discipline of self-flagellation. It is not depicted in Byzantine art and very rarely in the art of the Eastern Church. The column, to which Christ was tied during the ordeal, appears because it took place in Pilate's palace.

Little is known of the artist except that he worked mainly in Parma and Ravenna. His brother Bernardino also helped with this painting.

Christ is shown bust length, hair falling over his shoulders, with a crown of thorns on his head. A faint, delicately patterned halo can be seen. Behind is a square panel with foliated classical moulding. A noose is round his neck. The column is prominent and it is puzzling that in such scenes it should be so. The point of this close-up, as it were, simply a detail of the flagellation and mocking, is to aid Christian devotion. The viewer is brought close to look straight at a bare, vulnerable Christ. What the viewer sees is Christ's patient suffering and eyes that look with pity and reproach at what is happening.

In 2014, Her Majesty the Queen reflected:

'For me, the life of Jesus Christ, the Prince of Peace, is an inspiration and an anchor in my life. A role-model of reconciliation and forgiveness, he stretched out his hands in love, acceptance and healing.'

CHRIST AT THE COLUMN
Francesco Zaganelli
(c. 1470– 1532)
Royal Collection

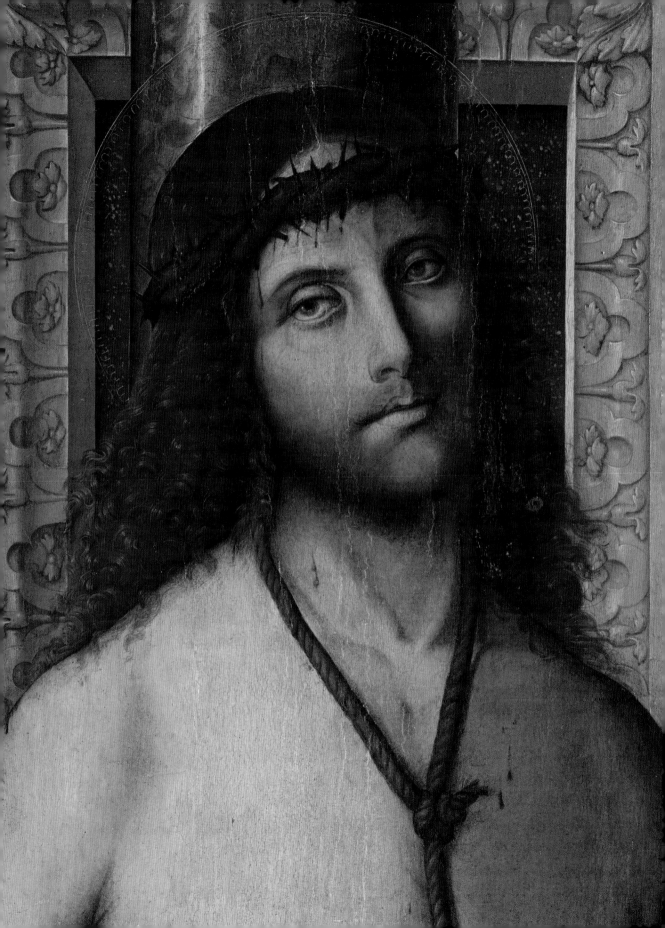

Jesus is crucified

So they took Jesus; and carrying the cross by himself, he went out to what is called The Place of the Skull, which in Hebrew is called Golgotha. There they crucified him and with him two others, one on either side, with Jesus between them . . .

Meanwhile, standing near the cross of Jesus were his mother, and his mother's sister, Mary the wife of Clopas, and Mary Magdalene. When Jesus saw his mother and the disciple whom he loved standing beside her, he said to his mother, 'Woman, here is your son.' Then he said to the disciple, 'Here is your mother.' And from that hour the disciple took her into his own home.

From the Gospel of John, chapter 19

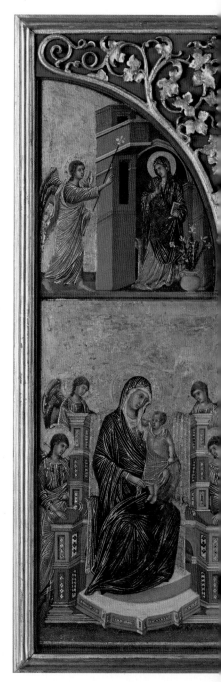

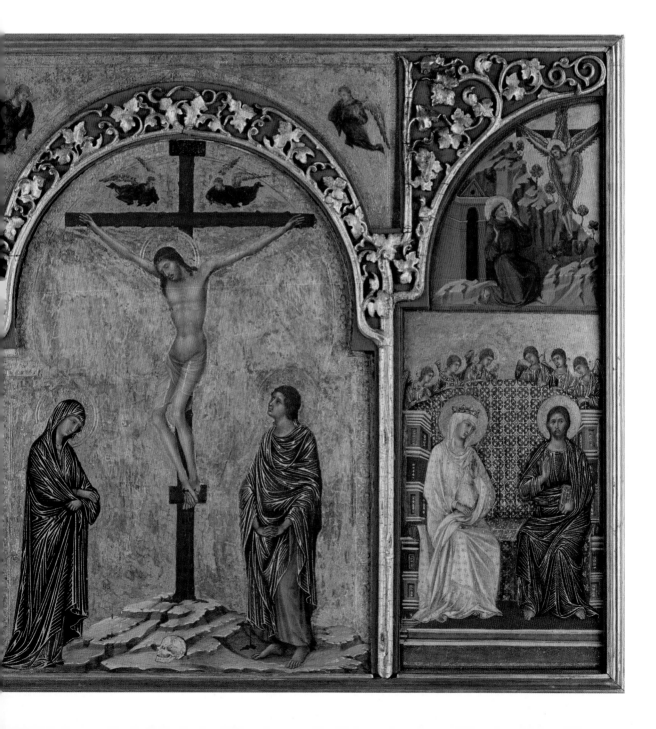

As mentioned earlier, Duccio lived and died in Siena, and worked mostly there and in the surrounding Tuscany area. His main work is a large, double-sided altarpiece for the cathedral in the city, the *Maestà*, which he worked on from 1308 to 1311. On the front of this is an enthroned Madonna with child and various smaller scenes. On the back are 46 panels on the life of Christ and his mother. The scenes on this superb painting in the Royal Collection shown here are closely related to those on the *Maestà* and it was worked on at the same time for a private patron. The difference is that, whereas the *Maestà* was for public viewing, this small triptych was for private devotion. For example, whereas the crucifixion scene on the *Maestà* is crowded, the triptych has only Mary and John standing before Christ in attitudes of devotion, drawing the viewer in to stand with them, either with head bowed like Mary or gazing up to Christ like John.

In this panel the cross stands on Golgotha, which according to tradition was where Adam was buried, whose skull is depicted. In Adam (meaning humanity as a whole), sin and death came to human beings; in Christ, the new humanity was born and given eternal life.

Around the main panel are four smaller ones: the annunciation, an enthroned Madonna with child, a crowned Madonna, and St Francis receiving the stigmata, indicating that the painting was commissioned by the Franciscans.

Duccio was influenced by both Byzantine painting and Cimabue, with the result that his

work has a strong devotional quality while at the same time developing the new Renaissance realism. As with Byzantine icons, he painted in egg tempera and used much gold. The influential fifteenth-century art critic Vasari thought that with Duccio and Giotto art had started to move away from what he described as the more primitive techniques of the Greeks. What we realize now though is that something was about to be lost. The work of Duccio still has a numinous quality which was no longer apparent in the High Renaissance.

The other influence on this panel is Franciscan spirituality. Francis and his followers encouraged people to read the Scriptures and look at religious pictures imagining that they were actually present in the scene, feeling all the appropriate emotions. So the friars and others who prayed before this triptych would have been encouraged to share in its tender prayerfulness.

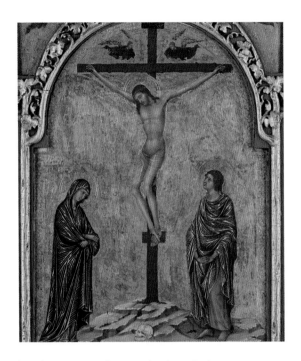

The cross stands on Golgotha, which according to tradition was where Adam was buried, whose skull is depicted. In Adam (meaning humanity as a whole), sin and death came to human beings; in Christ, the new humanity was born and given eternal life.

Jesus is mourned by his mother

Now there was a good and righteous man named
Joseph, who, though a member of the council,
had not agreed to their plan and action. He
came from the Jewish town of Arimathea, and
he was waiting expectantly for the kingdom of
God. This man went to Pilate and asked for the
body of Jesus. Then he took it down, wrapped it
in a linen cloth, and laid it in a rock-hewn tomb
where no one had ever been laid. It was the day
of Preparation, and the sabbath was beginning.
The women who had come with him from
Galilee followed, and they saw the tomb and
how his body was laid. Then they returned, and
prepared spices and ointments.
From the Gospel of Luke, chapter 23

PIETÀ
Gerard David (1455–1523)
King's Closet, Windsor Castle

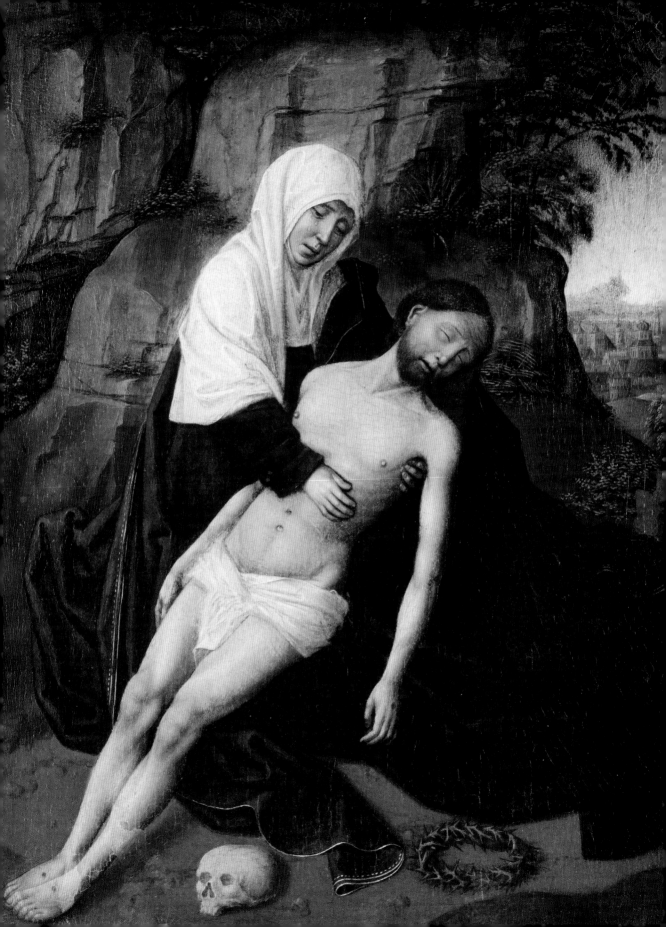

Gerard David was the leading artist of his time
in Bruges and he may have run a workshop in
Antwerp as well. Highly successful in his own
period, he fell out of favour in the seventeenth
century only to come back in again in the
nineteenth. It was then that his use of
colour and his ability with landscapes
were particularly valued.

The scenes after the crucifixion in art include
the lamentations and the Pietà, but the latter
usually depicts the body of Jesus lying across the
knee of his mother in an elegant pose. Here,
by contrast, the body of Jesus is shown stiff and
awkward to handle, for rigor mortis has set in.
Nevertheless the face of Mary looks tenderly
down and her hands gently hold the body. The
white of her scarf and the yellow body of Jesus
against a dark background give the scene a
slightly surreal quality. The light also picks out
a skull on the floor, the skull of Adam, the first
human being and symbol of the humanity Christ
came to redeem. Also on the floor is the plaited
crown of thorns. In the background are the
towers of Jerusalem.

In 2008, Her Majesty the Queen reflected:

'I hope that, like me, you will be comforted by the example of Jesus of Nazareth who, often in circumstances of great adversity, managed to live an outgoing, unselfish and sacrificial life . . . He makes it clear that genuine human happiness and satisfaction lie more in giving than receiving; more in serving than in being served. We can surely be grateful that, 2,000 years after the birth of Jesus, so many of us are able to draw inspiration from his life and message, and to find in him a source of strength and courage.'

5
EASTER GLORY

'The simple facts of Jesus' life give us little clue as to the influence he was to have on the world. His ministry only lasted a few years and he himself never wrote anything down. In his early thirties he was arrested, tortured and crucified with two criminals. His death might have been the end of the story, but then came the resurrection and with it the foundation of the Christian faith.'

The Queen's Christmas broadcast, 2000

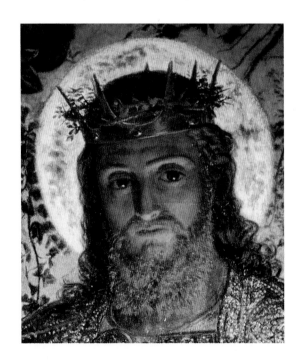

DETAIL FROM
THE LIGHT OF THE WORLD
Holman Hunt (1827–1910)
Keble College, Oxford

Christ is risen

When the sabbath was over, Mary Magdalene, and Mary the mother of James, and Salome bought spices, so that they might go and anoint him. And very early on the first day of the week, when the sun had risen, they went to the tomb. They had been saying to one another, 'Who will roll away the stone for us from the entrance to the tomb?' When they looked up, they saw that the stone, which was very large, had already been rolled back. As they entered the tomb, they saw a young man, dressed in a white robe, sitting on the right side; and they were alarmed. But he said to them, 'Do not be alarmed; you are looking for Jesus of Nazareth, who was crucified. He has been raised; he is not here. Look, there is the place they laid him. But go, tell his disciples and Peter that he is going ahead of you to Galilee; there you will see him, just as he told you.' So they went out and fled from the tomb, for terror and amazement had seized them; and they said nothing to anyone, for they were afraid.

From the Gospel of Mark, chapter 16

THE THREE MARYS FIND THE TOMB EMPTY AND CHRIST ASCENDS TO THE FATHER
Fifth-century ivory
Bayerisches Nationalmuseum, Munich

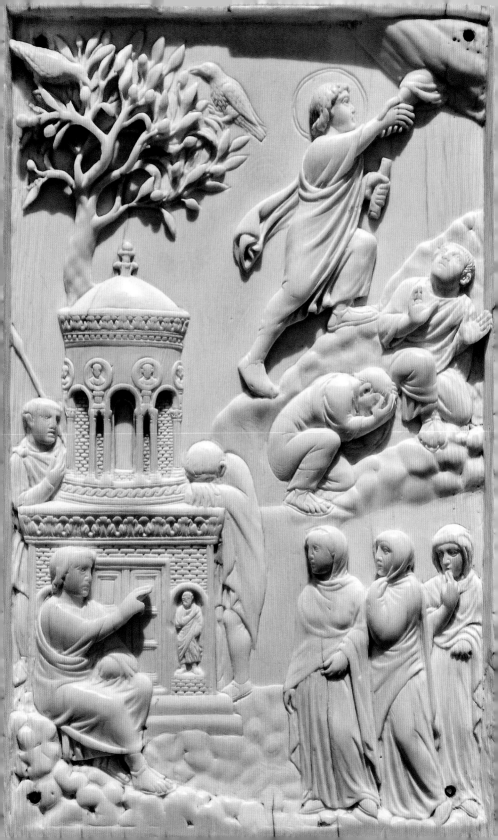

Some of the most evocative images we know of from the past are on ivory, for the simple reason that being durable they were more likely to survive. This one, which originated in Rome about the year 400, shows the three Marys arriving at the tomb and finding it empty. They are addressed by an angel who tells them that Christ is risen. The women are not shown here bearing spices, which they do according to the Gospel account and which later depictions of this scene show.

The tomb on the left is nothing like the rock tomb described in the Gospels. This is because when the Emperor Constantine became a Christian in the early fourth century he had a monument built over the place where Jesus was buried and from where he rose from the dead. What we have in this scene is this aedicule or small shrine which pilgrims to Jerusalem at the time would have seen. Today a successor to that monument can be seen in the Church of the Holy Sepulchre.

Behind the tomb are the two soldiers who were meant to be guarding it, one asleep or struck down with fear.

What is particularly interesting about this scene of the women finding the tomb empty is that it is combined not with a resurrection appearance, as we might have thought, but with the ascension. Jesus is being pulled into heaven by the hand of God, emphasizing the fact that 'he was taken up into heaven', as Mark and Luke stress. This combination of the finding of the tomb empty and the ascension very much accords with the perspective of John's Gospel, where the cross, the resurrection and the ascension are all part of one journey to the Father and one movement of divine glorification.

In the top left-hand corner a luxuriant tree is full of fruit and birds, symbolizing the flourishing that comes to the world with this new creation through the resurrection of Christ.

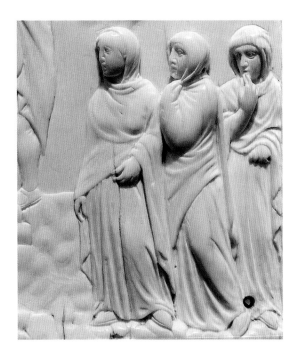

Some of the most evocative images we know
of from the past are on ivory . . . This one,
which originated in Rome about the year 400,
shows the three Marys arriving at the tomb
and finding it empty. They are addressed by
an angel who tells them that Christ is risen.

Jesus appears to Mary Magdalene

But Mary stood weeping outside the tomb. As she wept, she bent over to look into the tomb; and she saw two angels in white, sitting where the body of Jesus had been lying, one at the head and the other at the feet. They said to her, 'Woman, why are you weeping?' She said to them, 'They have taken away my Lord, and I do not know where they have laid him.' When she had said this, she turned round and saw Jesus standing there, but she did not know that it was Jesus. Jesus said to her, 'Woman, why are you weeping? For whom are you looking?' Supposing him to be the gardener, she said to him, 'Sir, if you have carried him away, tell me where you have laid him, and I will take him away.' Jesus said to her, 'Mary!' She turned and said to him in Hebrew, 'Rabbouni!' (which means Teacher). Jesus said to her, 'Do not hold on to me, because I have not yet ascended to the Father. But go to my brothers and say to them, "I am ascending to my Father and your Father, to my God and your God."' Mary Magdalene went and announced to the disciples, 'I have seen the Lord'; and she told them that he had said these things to her.

From the Gospel of John, chapter 20

**MARY MAGDALENE
AT THE TOMB**
Rembrandt (1606–69)
Royal Collection

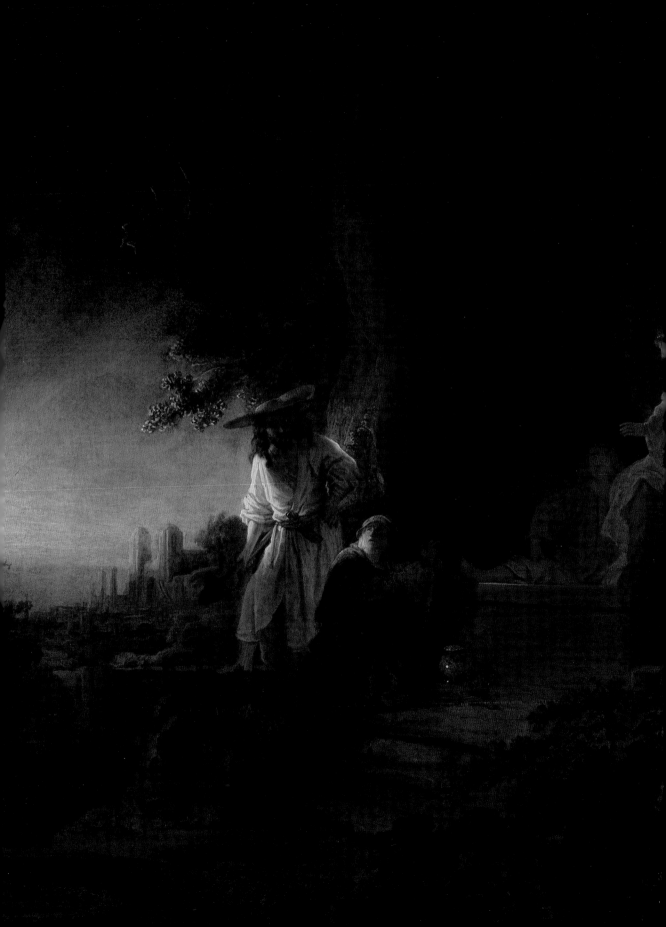

The mood and theme of this painting is set by the dawn which is just breaking. The light is coming from the distance, showing up the towers of Jerusalem but leaving much of the scene, under the tree, in semi-darkness. The light, however, picks out most of the figure of Jesus, the half-turned face of Mary and one of the angels. Unlike most artists who liked to paint the moment when Jesus says to Mary, *Noli me tangere*, or 'Do not cling on to me', as in the one by Titian below, Rembrandt has tried to capture the dawning realization before the full recognition. Mary half turns and sees a figure there whom she supposes is the gardener. It is only when he says her name that recognition comes. The spiritual dawning reflects the physical dawn; the half-light of the scene and the half-light of religious insight matching one another.

In the early centuries there was some reluctance to depict Mary Magdalene, in the belief that it should be Mary, the mother of Jesus, who should be central. By the eleventh century, however, there was no such hesitation and something of a cult of Mary Magdalene grew up. She is shown here in her traditional red cloak and long hair, reaching out to hold on to Jesus. The prominent tree almost mid-point in the painting divides the earthly from the heavenly, to which the risen Christ is withdrawing. The buildings of Jerusalem and Mary kneeling are the world we know. But to the left of the painting there is a sense of distance, a horizon opening up, light dawning.

There is a fine example of this scene by Giotto in the Scrovegni Chapel in Padua. In that and in this one by Titian we have an example of contrapposto, which has been defined as 'leaning towards her he also withdraws'. Traditionally the words *Noli me tangere* have been translated as 'Do not touch me', but it is better understood as 'Do not cling on to me'. Earlier in the Gospel, Christ had promised his followers his presence in the Spirit in a way which would be with them for ever. Mary is told that this appearance to her is not that permanent presence, 'because I have not *yet* ascended to the Father'. That will come when he has gone to the Father, when he will be present as God is present, at all times and in all places.

NOLI ME TANGERE
Titian (1488/90–1576)
The National Gallery, London

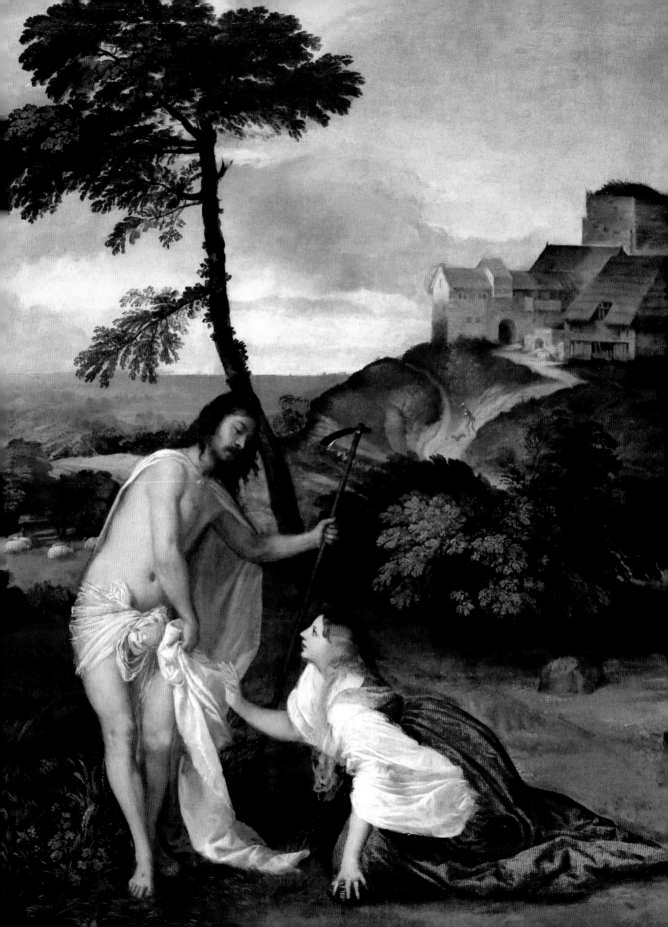

The disciple who doubted

DOUBTING THOMAS
Early eleventh-century mosaic
Osios Loukas, Greece

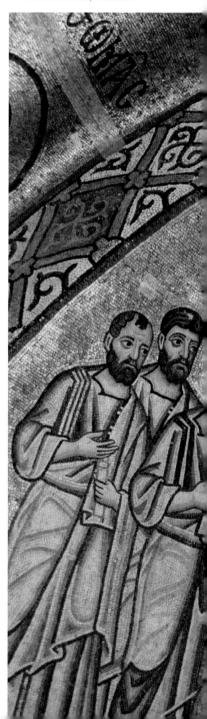

When it was evening on that day, the first day of the week, and the doors of the house where the disciples had met were locked for fear of the Jews, Jesus came and stood among them and said, 'Peace be with you.' After he said this, he showed them his hands and his side. Then the disciples rejoiced when they saw the Lord. Jesus said to them again, 'Peace be with you. As the Father has sent me, so I send you.' When he had said this, he breathed on them and said to them, 'Receive the Holy Spirit. If you forgive the sins of any, they are forgiven them; if you retain the sins of any, they are retained.'

But Thomas (who was called the Twin), one of the twelve, was not with them when Jesus came. So the other disciples told him, 'We have seen the Lord.' But he said to them, 'Unless I see the mark of the nails in his hands, and put my finger in the mark of the nails and my hand in his side, I will not believe.'

A week later his disciples were again in the house, and Thomas was with them. Although the doors were shut, Jesus came and stood among them and said, 'Peace be with you.' Then he said to Thomas, 'Put your finger here and see my hands. Reach out your hand and put it in my side. Do not doubt but believe.' Thomas answered him, 'My Lord and my God!' Jesus said to him, 'Have you believed because you have seen me? Blessed are those who have not seen and yet have come to believe.'

From the Gospel of John, chapter 20

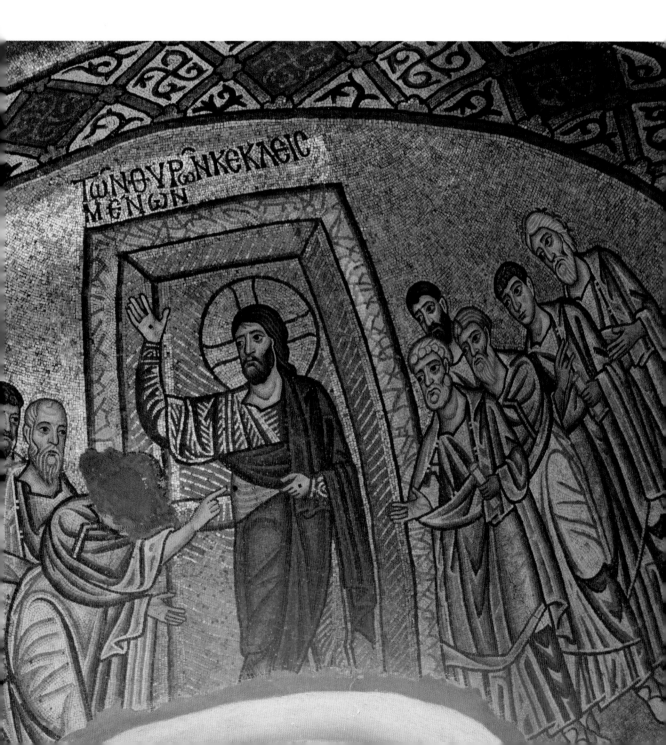

The small monastery of Osios Loukas, on the
north of the Gulf of Corinth in Greece, is a
gem. Unassuming from the outside, it contains
superb mosaics from a fine period of Byzantine
art. The Gospel tells us that Thomas was not
present at the first appearance of the risen Christ
to the disciples and doubted its truth. Here Christ
appears again and offers Thomas a chance to see
the wounds. He holds his hand up and pulls aside
the robe covering his side. Thomas (his face badly
damaged) holds out his hand and points his finger
at the side of Christ, though not in the dramatic
manner later depicted by Caravaggio. The other
ten Apostles look on, Judas no longer being of
their number.

Christ in the centre appears against a
background which is both a door and a
sarcophagus. The words above the door read in
translation, 'The doors being shut', from John
chapter 20. The door is the shut door which
cannot keep Christ out, the grave which cannot
hold him, and the entry into eternal life.

In April 2021, when the world was struck down by the Covid-19 virus, Her Majesty the Queen reflected:

'The discovery of the risen Christ on the first Easter Day gave his followers new hope and fresh purpose, and we can all take heart from this. We know that Coronavirus will not overcome us. As dark as death can be – particularly for those suffering with grief – light and life are greater. May the living flame of the Easter hope be a steady guide as we face the future.'

On the road to Emmaus

Now on that same day two of them were going to a village called Emmaus, about seven miles from Jerusalem, and talking with each other about all these things that had happened. While they were talking and discussing, Jesus himself came near and went with them, but their eyes were kept from recognizing him. And he said to them, 'What are you discussing with each other while you walk along?' They stood still, looking sad. Then one of them, whose name was Cleopas, answered him, 'Are you the only stranger in Jerusalem who does not know the things that have taken place there in these days?' He asked them, 'What things?' They replied, 'The things about Jesus of Nazareth, who was a prophet mighty in deed and word before God and all the people, and how our chief priests and leaders handed him over to be condemned to death and crucified him. But we had hoped that he was the one to redeem Israel. Yes, and besides all this, it is now the third day since these things took place. Moreover, some women of our group astounded us. They were at the tomb early this morning, and when they did not find his body there, they came back and told us that they had indeed seen a vision of angels who said that he was alive. Some of those who were with us went to the tomb and found it just as the women had said; but they did not see him.' Then he said to them, 'Oh, how foolish you are, and how slow of heart to believe all that the prophets have declared! Was it not necessary that the Messiah should suffer these things and then enter into his glory?' Then beginning with Moses and all the prophets, he interpreted to them the things about himself in all the scriptures.

From the Gospel of Luke, chapter 24

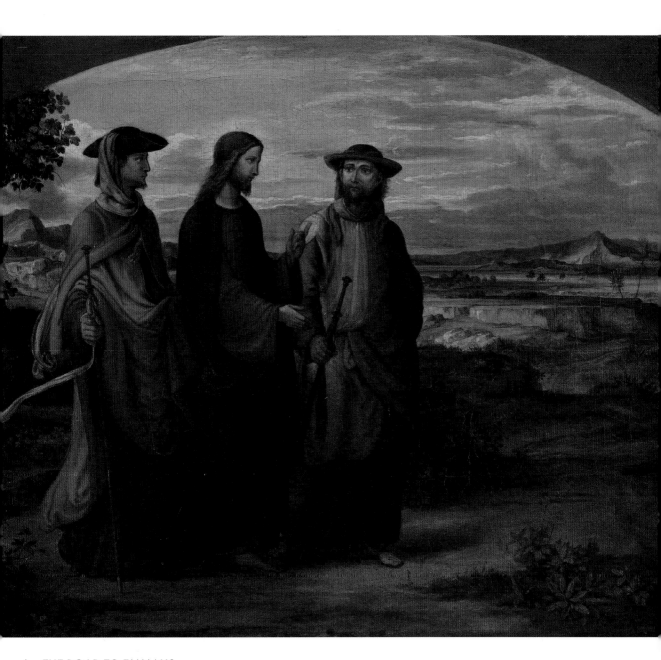

THE ROAD TO EMMAUS
Ferdinand Oliver (1785–1841)
Queen's sitting room,
Osborne House

The artist Ferdinand Oliver, who was born
in Switzerland, became a member of the
Nazarenes, a movement that wanted to revive
the more religiously inspired art of an earlier
age. They were nicknamed Nazarenes because
of their long hair and flowing robes based on a
verse in the Bible (Numbers chapter 6). Oliver
painted many biblical subjects and was
particularly interested in landscape as a
means of expressing Christian iconography.
The landscape here recalls that of Salzburg.

In this scene, two disciples, one called Cleopas,
were walking to Emmaus when they were joined
by a stranger with whom they talked about the
recent happenings in Jerusalem. The stranger,
later revealed to be the risen Christ, is shown
in a blue robe teaching them, as we can see by
his gesticulating hands. The two disciples are
listening carefully. The light of the sky reflected
in the landscape and on the three figures
indicates something ethereal. The three people
clearly belong to our ordinary everyday world
with its rough road; at the same time they seem
to belong to another surreal dimension.

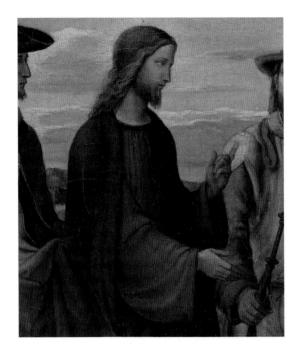

Two disciples, one called Cleopas, were walking
to Emmaus when they were joined by a stranger
with whom they talked about the recent happenings
in Jerusalem. The stranger, later revealed to be
the risen Christ, is shown in a blue robe teaching
them, as we can see by his gesticulating hands.

The supper at Emmaus

THE SUPPER AT EMMAUS
Attributed to Jacopo
Bassano (1510–92)
Royal Collection

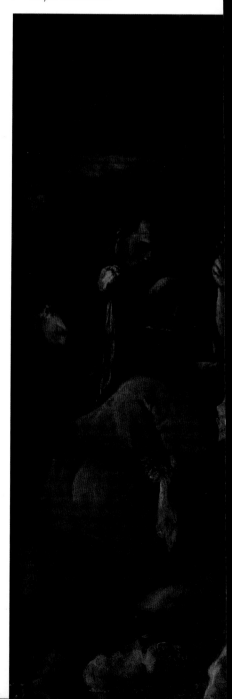

As they came near the village to which they were going, he walked ahead as if he were going on. But they urged him strongly, saying, 'Stay with us, because it is almost evening and the day is now nearly over.' So he went in to stay with them. When he was at the table with them, he took bread, blessed and broke it, and gave it to them. Then their eyes were opened, and they recognized him; and he vanished from their sight. They said to each other, 'Were not our hearts burning within us while he was talking to us on the road, while he was opening the scriptures to us?' That same hour they got up and returned to Jerusalem; and they found the eleven and their companions gathered together. They were saying, 'The Lord has risen indeed, and he has appeared to Simon!' Then they told what had happened on the road, and how he had been made known to them in the breaking of the bread.

From the Gospel of Luke, chapter 24

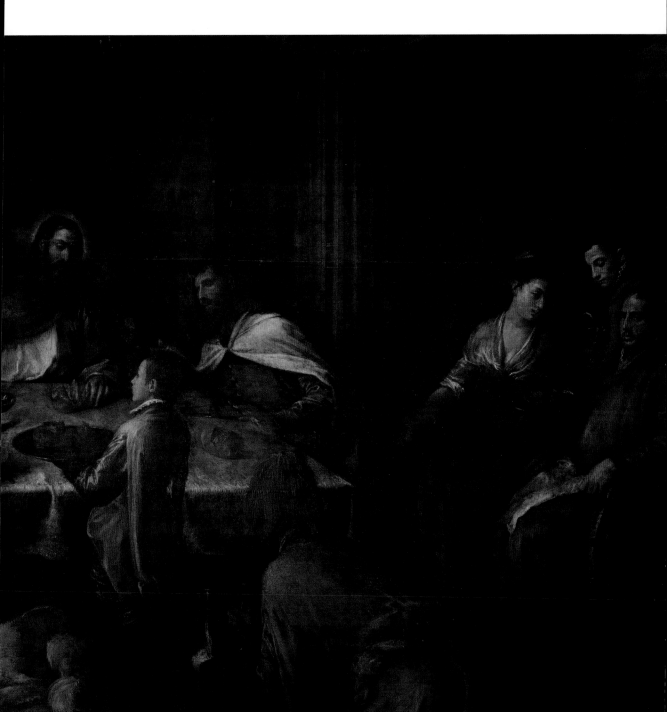

Bassano lived and worked in a village near
Venice, where he inherited a family workshop,
which his sons eventually took over from him. He
was influenced not only by the great Venetian
painters of the time but those from other parts of
Europe, even though he never travelled outside
his own region. He was best known for, and
popular as, a genre artist, including the faces
of local people and scenes from everyday life
in his work. We see this in his depiction of the
supper at Emmaus. To the right, the innkeeper
sits relaxed with other guests round him, talking
among themselves. To the bottom left is a dog
and cat. A servant boy brings a large dish of
food, while another in the foreground kneels
astonished. To the right of Christ, two onlookers
listen and bow their heads.

Christ holds one hand up in blessing and the
other on a loaf of bread. The two travellers,
one on Christ's left and one opposite him
on the right, listen attentively, though they
appear to be looking at each other rather than
Christ himself, as though they are querying
with one another as to what this all means.
Christ himself is shown as an ordinary host,
not a supernatural figure. This is, in the words
of George Herbert, 'heaven in ordinary'.

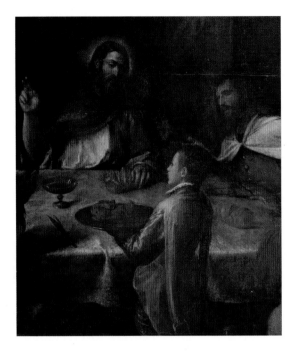

Christ holds one hand up in blessing and the
other on a loaf of bread. The two travellers,
one on Christ's left and one opposite him on
the right, listen attentively, though they appear
to be looking at each other rather than Christ
himself, as though they are querying with
one another as to what this all means.

'Feed my sheep'

CHRIST'S CHARGE TO PETER
Raphael 1483–1520
Royal Collection in the Victoria
and Albert Museum

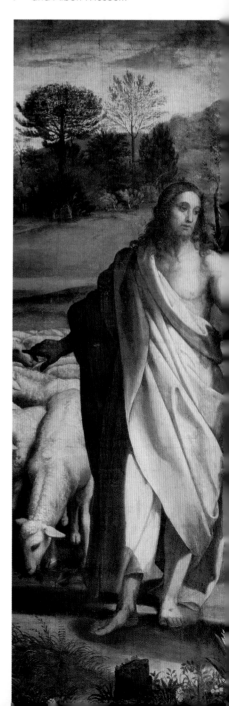

When they had finished breakfast, Jesus said to
Simon Peter, 'Simon son of John, do you love me
more than these?' He said to him, 'Yes, Lord; you
know that I love you.' Jesus said to him, 'Feed
my lambs.' A second time he said to him, 'Simon
son of John, do you love me?' He said to him,
'Yes, Lord; you know that I love you.' Jesus said
to him, 'Tend my sheep.' He said to him the third
time, 'Simon son of John, do you love me?' Peter
felt hurt because he said to him the third time,
'Do you love me?' And he said to him, 'Lord, you
know everything; you know that I love you.' Jesus
said to him, 'Feed my sheep.'
From the Gospel of John, chapter 21

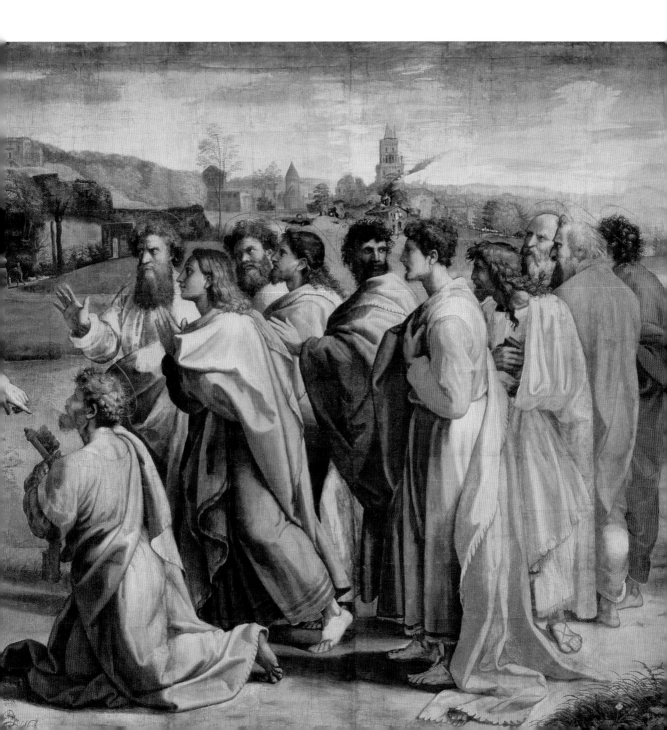

This is another large-scale drawing for the
tapestry in the Sistine Chapel. The setting is
the shore of the lake of Galilee after Christ's
resurrection, which Raphael depicts as a beautiful
landscape. The 11 Apostles are gathered together,
11 not 12 as Judas is no longer with them. Christ
addresses Peter, who is kneeling on the ground
looking imploringly at him. In Peter's mind is
the knowledge that three times he had denied his
Lord. Now he is given three chances to affirm his
love. Each time when he does this he is charged
to care for Christ's flock, the first congregation
of Christians. The point is reinforced pictorially
by the way that Christ's right hand points to
an actual flock of sheep behind him. In being
allowed to assure Christ of his love, and being
given this pastoral charge, Peter knows that he is
forgiven and trusted by his master. In his hands
are the keys of the kingdom of heaven, indicating
his huge new responsibility.

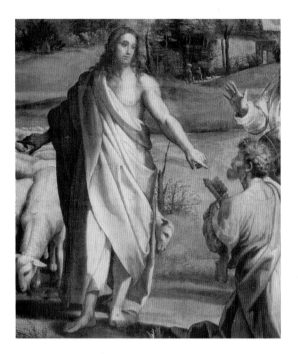

Christ addresses Peter, who is kneeling on the ground looking imploringly at him. In Peter's mind is the knowledge that three times he had denied his Lord. Now he is given three chances to affirm his love.

Anastasis

But someone will ask, 'How are the dead raised? With what kind of body do they come?' Fool! What you sow does not come to life unless it dies. And as for what you sow, you do not sow the body that is to be, but a bare seed, perhaps of wheat or of some other grain. But God gives it a body as he has chosen, and to each kind of seed its own body. Not all flesh is alike, but there is one flesh for human beings, another for animals, another for birds, and another for fish. There are both heavenly bodies and earthly bodies, but the glory of the heavenly is one thing, and that of the earthly is another. There is one glory of the sun, and another glory of the moon, and another glory of the stars; indeed, star differs from star in glory.

So it is with the resurrection of the dead. What is sown is perishable, what is raised is imperishable. It is sown in dishonour, it is raised in glory. It is sown in weakness, it is raised in power. It is sown a physical body, it is raised a spiritual body. If there is a physical body, there is also a spiritual body. Thus it is written, 'The first man, Adam, became a living being'; the last Adam became a life-giving spirit. But it is not the spiritual that is first, but the physical, and then the spiritual. The first man was from the earth, a man of dust; the second man is from heaven. As was the man of dust, so are those who are of the dust; and as is the man of heaven, so are those who are of heaven. Just as we have borne the image of the man of dust, we will also bear the image of the man of heaven.

What I am saying, brothers and sisters, is this: flesh and blood cannot inherit the kingdom of God, nor does the perishable inherit the imperishable. Listen, I will tell you a mystery! We will not all die, but we will all be changed, in a moment, in the twinkling of an eye, at the last trumpet. For the trumpet will sound, and the dead will be raised imperishable, and we will be changed. For this perishable body must put on imperishability, and this mortal body must put on immortality. When this perishable body puts on imperishability, and this mortal body puts on immortality, then the saying that is written will be fulfilled:

'Death has been swallowed up in victory.'
'Where, O death, is your victory?
Where, O death, is your sting?'

The sting of death is sin, and the power of sin is the law. But thanks be to God, who gives us the victory through our Lord Jesus Christ.

Therefore, my beloved, be steadfast, immovable, always excelling in the work of the Lord, because you know that in the Lord your labour is not in vain.

From St Paul's first letter to the Corinthians, chapter 15

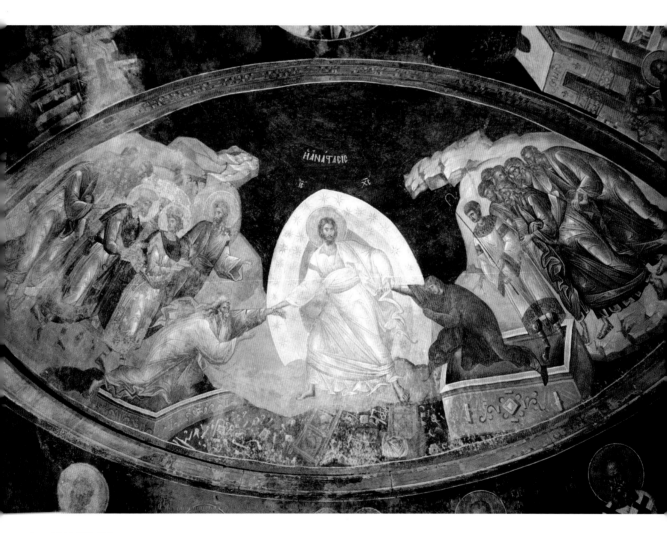

ANASTASIS
Fourteenth-century fresco
The mortuary chapel of
Chora Church, now the
Kariye Mosque in Istanbul

In the fourteenth century, Constantinople and its former empire were reduced to almost nothing, and in 1453 it was to be captured by Muslim forces. But this beleaguered period also saw one of the flowerings of Byzantine art under the Palaiologan dynasty. One of its fruits is the Chora Church, seen both in the beautiful mosaics in the main church and in this fresco of the Anastasis, the Greek word for resurrection, in the side chapel which was used for family funerals. It depicts Christ trampling on the gates and bars of hell. He is enclosed in an almond-shaped mandorla, spangled with stars and in three shades indicating the Trinity. To the viewer's left, Adam, and on the right, Eve, symbolizing humanity both male and female, are being pulled from their graves. Behind Adam, John the Baptist as the forerunner points to Christ, while behind him stand King Solomon and his father King David, symbolizing the human ancestry of Christ. On the viewer's right, with a shepherd's staff, is Abel, the first person to be killed and the first to rise from the dead. In the West this scene is called 'The descent to hell' and it finds its biblical basis in St Peter's first letter, chapter 3:

> For Christ also suffered for sins once for all, the righteous for the unrighteous, in order to bring you to God. He was put to death in the flesh, but made alive in the spirit, in which also he went and made a proclamation to the spirits in prison, who in former times did not obey, when God waited patiently in the days of Noah, during the building of the ark, in which a few, that is, eight people, were saved through water.

In the early centuries this theme was supplemented by stories in the apocryphal Gospels and this in turn gave rise to a rich literary tradition based on them.

In Western painting, the resurrection of Christ is usually treated rather simplistically, with his body shown rising out of the tomb. The East was much more concerned with the real meaning of the event, Christ's victory over evil and death, and it is this which is shown in the Anastasis. Christ's resurrection, his unbroken union with the Father, even in the darkness of sin, has universal significance, for in him that union is shared with the whole world and all creation. So, as Paul wrote:

> 'Death has been swallowed up in victory.'
> 'Where, O death, is your victory?
> Where, O death, is your sting?'

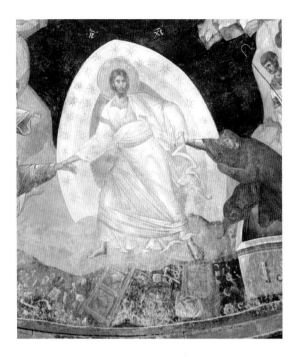

This fresco of the Anastasis, the Greek word
for resurrection, . . . depicts Christ trampling on
the gates and bars of hell. He is enclosed in
an almond-shaped mandorla, spangled with
stars and in three shades indicating the Trinity.

Christ in glory

Around the throne, and on each side of the
throne, are four living creatures, full of eyes in
front and behind: the first living creature like a
lion, the second living creature like an ox, the
third living creature with a face like a human
face, and the fourth living creature like a flying
eagle. And the four living creatures, each of them
with six wings, are full of eyes all around and
inside. Day and night without ceasing they sing,

> 'Holy, holy, holy,
> the Lord God the Almighty,
> who was and is and is to come.'

And whenever the living creatures give glory
and honour and thanks to the one who is seated
on the throne, who lives for ever and ever, the
twenty-four elders fall before the one who is
seated on the throne and worship the one who
lives for ever and ever; they cast their crowns
before the throne, singing,

> 'You are worthy, our Lord and God,
> to receive glory and honour and power,
> for you created all things,
> and by your will they existed
> and were created.'

From the book of Revelation, chapter 4

**CHRIST IN GLORY IN
THE TETRAMORPH**
Graham Sutherland (1903–80)
Coventry Cathedral

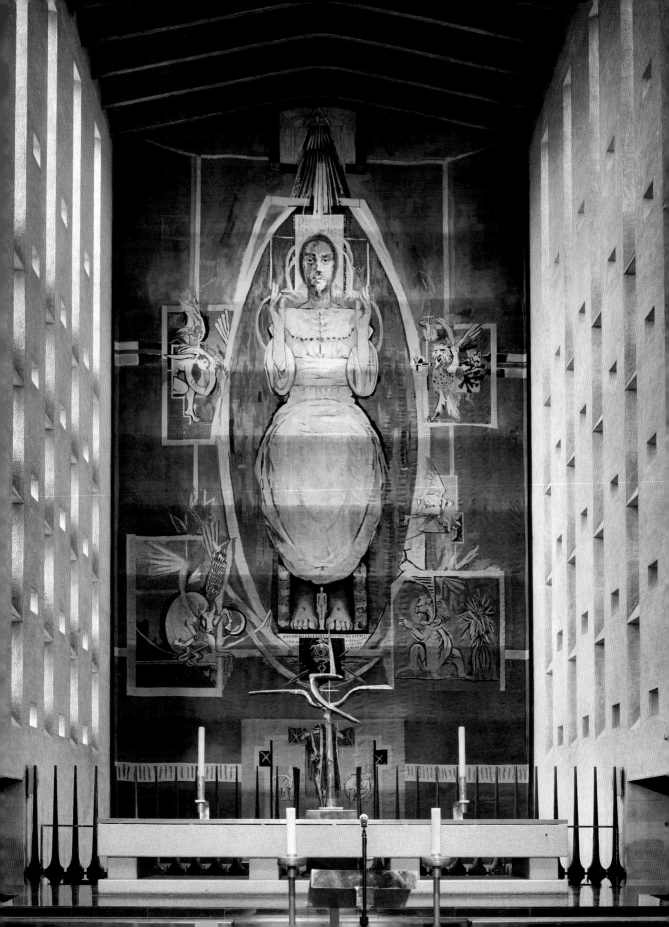

As Coventry Cathedral was badly bombed in the Second World War it was decided to build a new cathedral beside the ruins of the old one. Consecrated in 1963, although it was modernist in many ways, in terms of its shape it was the last of the medieval cathedrals in the sense that it has a long nave looking towards the altar. The new Roman Catholic cathedral in Liverpool, consecrated in 1967, was by contrast built in the round, reflecting the new understanding of liturgy. The long nave in Coventry has the advantage that the eye of anyone entering is drawn towards the scene of Christ in glory at the North End. The tetramorphs are the four creatures described in Revelation 4, which were early taken to be the signs of the four Evangelists, the lion for St Mark, the eagle for St John, the ox for St Luke and the winged man or angel for St Matthew. Graham Sutherland loved painting the angular shapes found in nature, such as thorn bushes, and this finds expression here.

Below the main figure is a small but very fine crucifix. Graham Sutherland, a Roman Catholic convert, had originally made a name for himself as a modern religious painter with his crucifixion for St Matthew's, Northampton, to which this is related. Above the crucifix a tiny human stands between the large feet of Christ, who sits in glory on the throne in an almond mandorla, hands and arms pointing heavenwards but at the same time indicating a sense of holding, of cradling the whole world in his arms. The colours of the tapestry are striking.

The tapestry was woven in France on a 500-year-old loom and took 12 weavers 2 years to make. It used blocks of 900 different colours to obtain different shades. Measuring 23x12 metres, it weighs a ton.

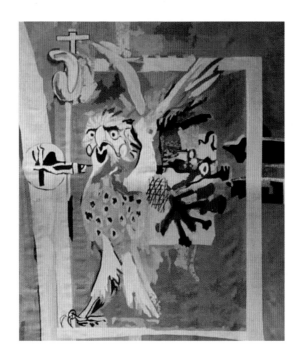

The tetramorphs are the four creatures described
in Revelation 4, which were early taken to be the
signs of the four Evangelists, the lion for St Mark, the
eagle for St John (shown here), the ox for St Luke
and the winged man or angel for St Matthew.

Christ close to every human heart

'Listen! I am standing at the door, knocking; if
you hear my voice and open the door, I will come
in to you and eat with you, and you with me. To
the one who conquers I will give a place with me
on my throne, just as I myself conquered and sat
down with my Father on his throne. Let anyone
who has an ear listen to what the Spirit is saying
to the churches.'
From the book of Revelation, chapter 3

THE LIGHT OF THE WORLD
Holman Hunt (1827–1910)
Keble College, Oxford

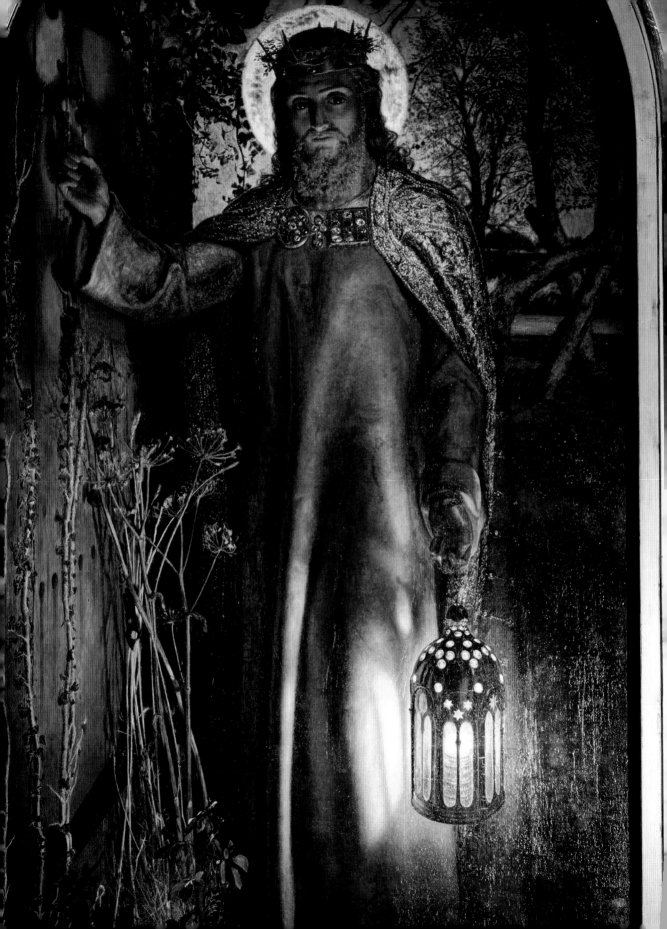

Holman Hunt began this painting when he was
20 but delayed finishing it until he had seen what
he thought of as a perfect dawn in Bethlehem.
The morning star arises above the head of Jesus.
A small version of the painting is in Manchester
and a larger one, painted when Holman Hunt
was 70, hangs in St Paul's Cathedral.

Although the Victorian age saw the rise of
agnosticism it was a period dominated by intense
religious fervour as a result of the continuing
influence of the Evangelical movement and the
growing strength of Anglo-Catholicism, also
known as the Oxford Movement. This painting
became something of an icon for Christians of
all opinions, although Hunt himself, as one of the
group known as Pre-Raphaelites who sought to
recover the traditions of the fourteenth century,
was an Anglo-Catholic. When the St Paul's
version went on a world tour in 1905–7 it drew
large crowds and it was estimated that four-fifths
of the population of Australia saw it.

Under the painting are words from Revelation
chapter 3 in the Authorised Version: 'Behold, I
stand at the door and knock; if any man hear
my voice, and open the door, I will come in to
him, and will sup with him, and he with me.'
In the painting, the door, which has been long
shut, is overgrown by vegetation and has no door
handle. It has to be opened from the inside. On
the outside, Christ the light of the world stands
with lantern, his hand knocking on the door. The
dawn rises, corresponding to what will happen in
the human soul as it opens the door.

Her Majesty the Queen has said:

'The teachings of Christ have served as my inner light, as has the sense of purpose we can find in coming together in worship.'

In 2002, she reflected:

'I know just how much I rely on my faith to guide me through the good times and the bad. Each day is a new beginning. I know that the only way to live my life is to try to do what is right, to take the long view, to give of my best in all that the day brings, and to put my trust in God. I draw strength from the message of hope in the Christian gospel.'

Picture credits

Royal Collection Trust / © His Majesty King Charles III 2023 (pages 5, 14, 17, 21, 29, 31, 32, 33, 41, 49, 53, 57, 127, 133, 135, 139, 149, 157, 161, 165)

Visitation by Rogier van der Weyden (c. 1435), Museum der bildenden Künste, Leipzig, Saxony, Germany © Azoor Collection / Alamy Stock Photo (page 9)

Nativity of the Lord, icon by St Andrei Rublev (1405), Cathedral of the Annunciation, Moscow Kremlin, Russia © Niday Picture Library / Alamy Stock Photo (page 13)

The Sleeping Magi, capital column (twelfth century), Autun Cathedral, Autun, Saone-et-Loire, Burgundy, France © Ivan Vdovin / Alamy Stock Photo (page 27)

Twelve-year-old Jesus in the Temple by Albrecht Dürer (1497) © FineArt / Alamy Stock Photo (page 35)

Christ in the House of His Parents ('The Carpenter's Shop') by John Everett Millais (c. 1849), oil on canvas © Ian Dagnall Computing / Alamy Stock Photo (page 37)

Christ in the Wilderness by Briton Rivière (1898 (1912)) © The Print Collector / Alamy Stock Photo (page 45)

Jesus Healing the Bleeding Woman, detail from a Roman sarcophagus, early Christian (fourth century), Vatican Museums, Vatican City © Lanmas / Alamy Stock Photo (page 49)

The Calling of St Matthew by Michelangelo Caravaggio (c. 1598–1601), oil on panel, Contarelli Chapel, San Luigi dei Francesi, Rome, Italy © History & Art Collection / Alamy Stock Photo (page 61)

Walking on Water III by Roger Wagner, reproduced by courtesy of the artist, Roger Wagner

The Good Samaritan by Rembrandt van Rijn (1630), Wallace Collection, London © Peter Barritt / Alamy Stock Photo (page 69)

The Parable of the Mote and the Beam by Domenico Fetti (c. 1619) © CBW / Alamy Stock Photo (page 73)

The Sower (Sower at Sunset) by Vincent Van Gogh (1888) © Niday Picture Library / Alamy Stock Photo (page 77)

Kitchen Scene with Christ in the House of Martha and Mary by Diego Velázquez (c. 1618), oil on canvas © Ian Dagnall Computing / Alamy Stock Photo (page 81)

The Raising of Lazarus by Duccio di Buoninsegna (1310–11) © The Artchives / Alamy Stock Photo (page 85)

Christ and the Woman Taken in Adultery by Max Beckmann © Artepics / Alamy Stock Photo (page 89)

Christ Blessing the Children by Artemisia Gentileschi (c. 1624–55), Basilica dei Santi Ambrogio e Carlo al Corso, Rome, Italy © Album / Alamy Stock Photo (page 93)

Return of the Prodigal Son by Rembrandt van Rijn (c. 1663–5), oil on canvas © Ian Dagnall Computing / Alamy Stock Photo (page 97)

The Transfiguration, sixth-century mosaic © St Catherine's Monastery, Mt Sinai (page 101)

The Entry into Jerusalem, Church of Our Lady of the Pastures, Asinou, Cyprus © Sonia Halliday Photo Library / Alamy Stock Photo (page 107)

Christ Driving the Money-changers from the Temple by Dirck van Baburen (1621) © agefotostock / Alamy Stock Photo (page 111)

The Last Supper by Ugolino da Siena (1330) © FineArt / Alamy Stock Photo (page 115)

The Agony in the Garden of Gethsemane by El Greco (c. 1590) © incamerastock / Alamy Stock Photo (page 119)

The Betrayal of Christ by Judas Iscariot, fresco by Giotto (c. 1305), Scrovegni Chapel, Padua, Italy © Granger – Historical Picture Archive / Alamy Stock Photo (page 123)

Christ Mocked by Soldiers by Georges Rouault (1932), Museum of Modern Art, New York © Album / Alamy Stock Photo (page 131)

Women at the Tomb of Christ and the Ascension of the Lord, ivory plate, Milan or Rome (c. AD 400), National Museum, Munich © imageBROKER / Alamy Stock Photo (page 145)

Noli me tangere by Titian (c. 1514) © Niday Picture Library / Alamy Stock Photo (page 151)

Doubting Thomas, mosaic (c. 1011/1030), Katholikon church, Osios Loukas monastery, Greece © B. O'Kane / Alamy Stock Photo (page 153)

The Anastasis, fresco, Church of the Holy Saviour in Chora, Kariye Jami, Istanbul, Turkey © B. O'Kane / Alamy Stock Photo (page 169)

Christ in Glory, tapestry by Graham Sutherland (1962), Coventry Cathedral © Angelo Hornak / Alamy Stock Photo (page 173)

The Light of the World by Holman Hunt (c. 1851–4), Keble College, Oxford © John Bracegirdle / Alamy Stock Photo (page 177)

—

SEEING GOD IN ART

Read on for an extract from *Seeing God in Art* by Richard Harries

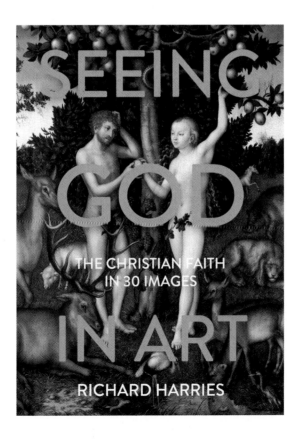

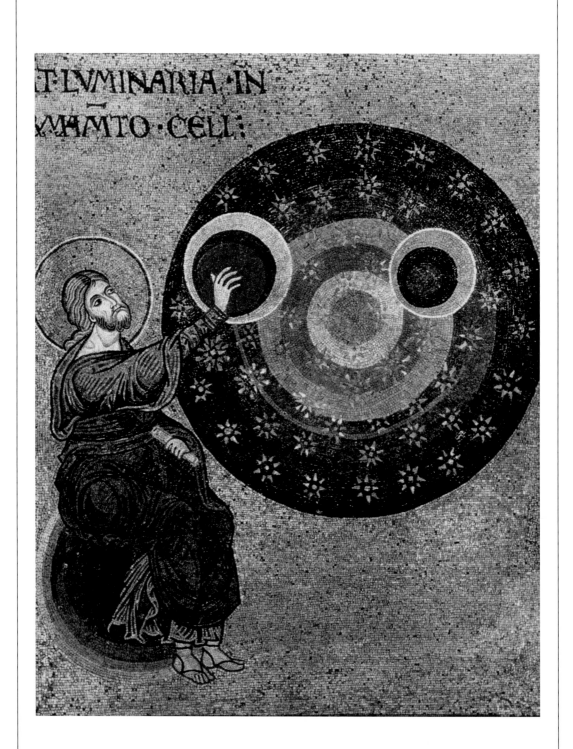

1

'Let there be . . .'

The creation of the sun, moon and stars, twelfth-century mosaic

This is one of the many superb mosaics in Monreale Cathedral, in Palermo, Sicily, that tell the Christian story from creation onwards. It depicts the creation of the stars, the sun and moon, and the planets (Genesis 1.1–5, 14–19). In God's left hand is a scroll that symbolizes the ruling principles on which the universe operates or, as we would say, the fundamental laws of nature. A similar scheme of mosaics can be found in the nearby Palatine chapel in the royal palace.

As mentioned in the Introduction, there was a difference between East and West in their understanding of Christian art. In these Monreale mosaics, the two approaches come together. The Christian story is told from creation onwards, but each scene has an iconic quality that draws us to reflect and pray.

The creation of the universe is of course beyond anything our tiny human minds can picture, but the artist here has made a bold attempt to put it in symbolic form. All stems from God's great 'Let there be . . .', indicated by his outstretched arm. This 'Let there be . . .' runs throughout the first chapter of the Bible. God's hand not only brings things into being, it is a hand that blesses. It reminds us of other words from Genesis: 'All that he made was very good'.

We might think it childlike to picture God in these terms, but however sophisticated our attempt to visualize the moment when matter appeared *ex nihilo*, out of nothing, it will still only be a human picture of what is beyond our comprehension. In a way, the more childlike the better, for it then brings home to us the fact that we are using human images to depict what cannot be imagined.

One of the great scientific achievements of recent decades is that the created side of this unimaginable moment of creation can be mapped out in mathematical terms. Advanced instruments for measurement, together with very high-level maths, can take astronomers and mathematical physicists back to the first few seconds of the explosion of energy we call the 'big bang': the point from which the universe has since expanded ever outwards at the speed of light. It was the Catholic priest and astronomer Georges Lemaître who first noted in 1927 that an expanding universe could be traced back in time to an originating single point; since then, scientists have built on his idea of cosmic expansion.

We now know that the universe is 13.8 billion years old. It contains 10 billion galaxies, and each galaxy contains about 100 billion stars. This means that there are something like one billion trillion stars in the observable universe. Earth is of course a planet of one star, the Sun, which is part of one galaxy, the Milky Way. Time and space, as we know them, begin at this point. No wonder the psalmist cries out, 'The heavens declare the glory of God: and the firmament sheweth his handywork' (Psalm 19.1, KJV). No wonder poets in every age, like Gerard Manley Hopkins, have written words such as 'The world is charged with the grandeur of God. / It will flame out, like shining from shook foil.' We do not know God in himself. We only know him in and through the secondary causes of which he is the first cause. We know him in the wonder we feel when we look up at the night sky.

What is fascinating about the brilliant scientific work done on the origin of the universe in recent decades is the way its truth has been yielded up through mathematical equations of great beauty. Mathematicians sometimes marvel at the way amazing complexity can be brought together in equations of such simplicity and elegance. Not unrelated to this phenomenon is the equally amazing capacity of the human mind to explore and map out the universe in this way. All this bears out what the Church has long taught, both about the fundamental beauty of the universe and the natural laws on which it is based, and our God-given reason, which is able to recognize and understand these laws.

No scientific exploration can locate God in this process, for God is not a thing in the world of things. He is the uncreated source of all things. There is only one place where we can discover God, and that is in ourselves. We discover him as the root of our own existence, the source from whom our being flows. But because the fundamental energy that keeps us in being is one with the fundamental energy that brought the universe into being in the first place, God is the root of the universe as well. Moment by moment I am held in being – and if I am, so is the universe as a whole.

That is what is really meant when we say that God is creator, and that is why it would not affect this belief if some scientific reality could be found to exist before the 'big bang'. That too would exist only because of the uncreated source of all energy. Nor would it affect the issue if it were discovered that there is a multiverse. Before the theory of the 'big bang' was shown to be true, a widely held view was that the universe was being continuously created. Even now it could be that the 'big bang' was just one in a series of explosions and contractions. If this were shown to be so, again it would not affect the fundamental Christian belief, shared by Jews and Muslims, that whatever the process whereby we come into being, it depends on an uncreated source of all processes. The basis of this belief is the lived faith of believers, that they are dependent on God as they are on the air they breathe and the ground they walk on.

Unimaginable God, you have set us in this universe of awesome grandeur. Moment by moment you hold it in existence. You are the fount from whom my being flows. On you I depend, in you I trust.

SISTER WENDY'S 100 BEST-LOVED PAINTINGS

Read on for an extract from *Sister Wendy's 100 Best-loved Paintings* by Sister Wendy Beckett

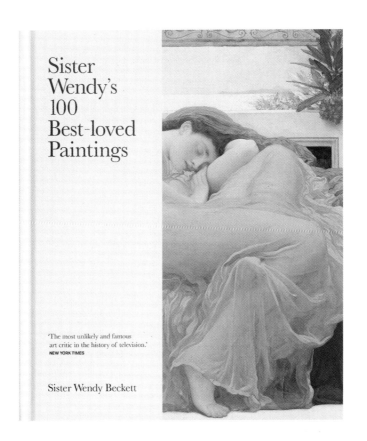

Sister
Wendy's
100
Best-loved
Paintings

'The most unlikely and famous
art critic in the history of television.'
NEW YORK TIMES

Sister Wendy Beckett

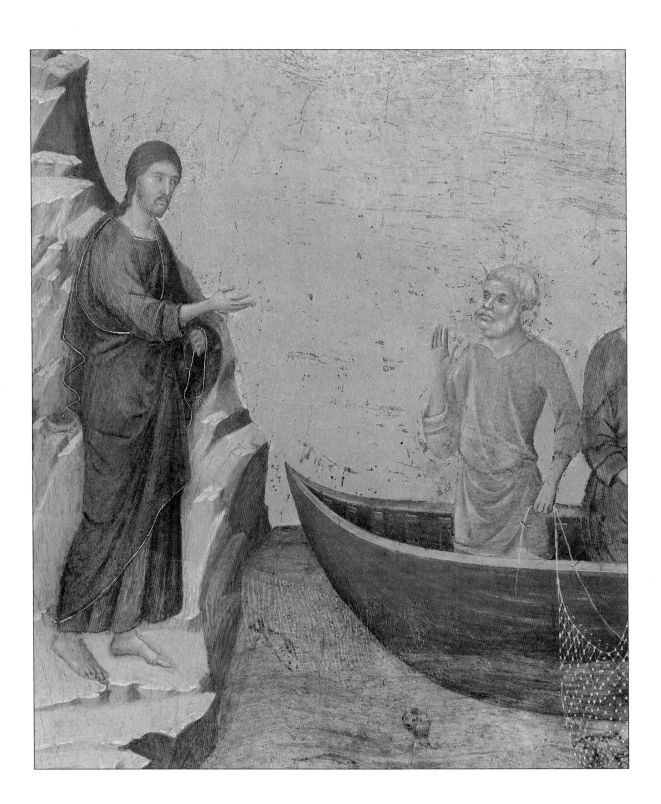

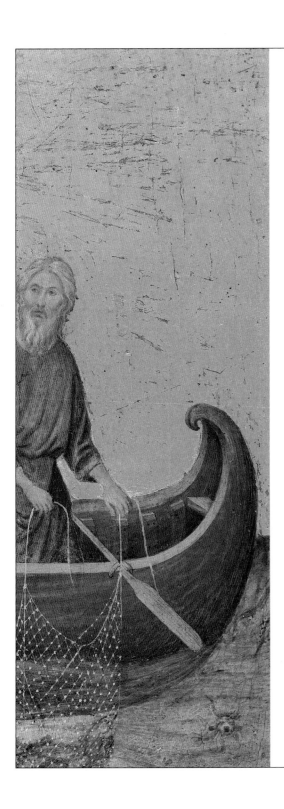

PART ONE
6th–14th centuries

Duccio,
*The Calling of
the Apostles
Peter and Andrew*
(1308–11)

1

—

VIRGIN
AND CHILD

6th or 7th century

Although I would not presume to call myself an art historian, I must confess to having shared in the art historical wariness of the icon. What liberated me from my near-sighted folly was the icon I saw in the Temple Gallery in London in 2003. Up to then books on Byzantine art or on icons in general had lamented that only seven icons of the Virgin had survived the period of iconoclasm. All seven were known, though by no means well known. What happened in 2003, however, meant that the history books had to be rewritten.

Dick Temple and Laurence Morrocco discovered in a small auction house in Avignon, France, a blackened and tattered encaustic image, which, they could recognize, was a very early icon of the Mother of God. The use of wax, which is what encaustic means, is limited to the early centuries, but it was the sheer power of the image itself that convinced Temple that he had found something of extraordinary significance. It is a painting on linen, and when it was discovered it was clumsily glued on to a rectangular piece of cardboard. It took the Temple Gallery two years to clean it and to consolidate it, two years also in which they sought to find its origin. The general consensus seems to be that it

hung in some church in Egypt during the sixth or seventh century and has miraculously survived to give us an unimaginably precious insight into the poetry of early Christian thinking.

The Virgin herself, with her oval face and swanlike neck, looks away from the viewer. Apart from a gold cross over her forehead, she is simply dressed in black and shades of brown. Her gentle removal of herself from our attention has been described as aloof, but it does not seem so to me. She is well aware of our presence, and by no means indifferent to it, but all that matters to her is that we should regard the little Jesus. The passion that is absent from her face is visible in the very firm grip with which she holds the mandorla.

A mandorla is almond-shaped, rather like a shield, and we find it surrounding the infant Jesus on many early icons. It has been wondered if there is a reference here to the shield on which the Roman emperor was accustomed to display his son to the waiting army. For the Christian, the son of the Roman emperor, his heir, has given place to the child Jesus, equally emperor, but in no worldly sense.

There is a striking seventh-century Virgin at the Monastery of St Catherine at Mount Sinai, which is so destroyed that it does not count among the surviving eight. We can still make out, though, that the Virgin holds her son enclosed in an oval shield that is bright red. Here, however, the shield or mandorla is transparent. We can see Mary's large and powerful hand grasping the rim, as she subdues herself completely to the reality of Jesus. Furthermore, as it is transparent, we can see through to the place of Mary's womb. This is her significance: that in her, God, the Word, became flesh.

'An unimaginably precious insight into the poetry of early Christian thinking.'

Extract from Sister Wendy's 100 Best-loved Paintings

Wonderful though I find this Madonna, what seems to be truly extraordinary is the depiction of Jesus. This is a child, an anxious child. He knows that there is an answer, but yet not what it is, and his big searching eyes implore us to join with him in his quest. He is small, but not a baby. He has a rough mop of red curls, dark eyes, and a strong masculine mouth. Here we can see a likeness to his mother: whose rosy lips are womanly, but very firm. In one hand he holds what may be a scroll, but we feel that perhaps he is independent of written wisdom.

This is a child alive with a passionate desire to seek the truth and pleading with us to join with him in this all-absorbing search. His small, sandalled feet dangle in human vulnerability as he shows himself to us, held and yet not held by his mother. She holds the mandorla, not the child. He is there for our possessing, human, unprotected and haunting, an image like no other.

2

CHRIST
PANTOCRATOR

6th century

From the eighth century until halfway through the ninth century, the Byzantine Empire set about destroying all its icons. Wherever holy images existed, they were burned, thrown into rivers, hacked to pieces, whitewashed if on walls, scribbled over if in books. From this iconoclastic fury hardly anything has survived. There are eight icons of the Virgin Mary, mostly kept safe in Rome where the Byzantine Emperor had no power, and for the rest there is only a pathetic and damaged number of ancient icons in the remote desert monastery of St Catherine. Supreme among these pre-iconoclastic images is this magnificent icon of Christ the Ruler of All, the Pantocrator.

The icon painter never invented, never inaugurated. The whole point of the icon was that it was true; this was a real image. The mandylion, said to have been miraculously imprinted on a cloth, set the standard for the icon of Jesus.[5] He is dark-haired, brown-eyed, he has a slight beard, a strong and powerful neck, and an air of majesty. This exceptionally early icon captures with grace and beauty what the early Christians saw as the essence of the Saviour.

In those far-off centuries, the truth of the faith was still imperilled. There were Christians who believed that there was only a divine Jesus, and the human Jesus was just a pretence. They could not face the reality of his physical presence. There were equally Christians who denied his full divinity and saw Jesus as the greatest of the prophets but not as the Son of God. This icon expresses that holy union of the two natures, divine and human. It was because Jesus was human that there could be icons made of him. In the sixth century there was a passionate need to establish the reality of the God-man of Christ the Pantocrator, the all-powerful.

Against a dimly glimpsed background of the real world – we can see mountains, fields, buildings, trees – Jesus stands erect. His great halo has been gilded, blotting out the sky with its brightness. In one hand he holds the book of the Gospels, glittering with gold and jewels and marked with a cross. This is the only reference in the icon to his sufferings. His other hand is raised in the traditional blessing, in which the fingers form the initials, in Greek, of his name: IC XC.

Extract from Sister Wendy's 100 Best-loved Paintings

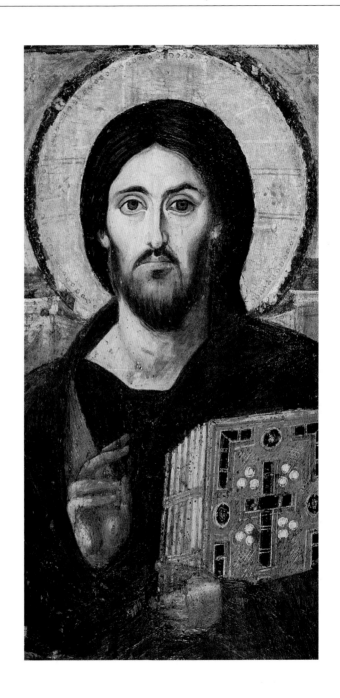

WE HAVE A VISION OF A WORLD IN WHICH EVERYONE IS TRANSFORMED BY CHRISTIAN KNOWLEDGE

As well as being an award-winning publisher, SPCK is the oldest Anglican mission agency in the world.

Our mission is to lead the way in creating books and resources that help everyone to make sense of faith.

Will you partner with us to put good books into the hands of prisoners, great assemblies in front of schoolchildren and reach out to people who have not yet been touched by the Christian faith?

To donate, please visit www.spckpublishing.co.uk/donate or call our friendly fundraising team on 020 7592 3900.